T0147960

On Giants' Shoulders
Beyond a Personal Myth

Simon J Watson

iUniverse, Inc.
New York   Bloomington

On Giants' Shoulders

Beyond a Personal Myth

iUniverse books may be ordered through booksellers or by contacting:

iUniverse
1663 Liberty Drive
Bloomington, IN 47403
www.iuniverse.com
1-800-Authors (1-800-288-4677)

ISBN: 978-1-4401-3555-2 (pbk)
ISBN: 978-1-4401-3569-9 (ebk)

Printed in the United States of America

iUniverse rev. date: 9/4/2009

"I should love to satisfy all, if I possibly can; but in trying to satisfy all, I may be able to satisfy none. I have, therefore, arrived at the conclusion that the best course is to satisfy one's own conscience and leave the world to form its own judgment, favorable or otherwise."

-Mohandas K. Gandhi
(1869-1948)

Dedicated To:

My wife Alice
For her love and constancy

My sons Andrew and Ryan
For their unabashed truths

My friend R.C. Bunger
For his fellowship and steadfastness

ACKNOWLEDGEMENTS

▼

Many people have played a role on the creation of this book, and not all of them can be listed here. My thanks and gratitude go to everyone who has helped me, directly and indirectly, and I will specifically acknowledge the following people, who have played a specific part:

Alice, my wife, and the life partner that every person dreams of, but few find.

Andrew and Ryan, my sons and buddies — and earnest advisors.

Doreen and Jerry, my parents, to whom I am eternally grateful for everything they did for me and my three siblings Mick, Lyndsey, and Robin.

RC Bunger, Fire Chief, Statistician, Professor, Attorney at Law, and warrior statesman: My dearest friend, and my greatest partner in this endeavor.

Tikie, my friend, colleague, and the person who showed me there can be enlightenment and integrity in business leadership.

Judeann, my friend, colleague and reluctant guru.

Ben, my friend, and the person who helped me see I could guide and be guided by the same person.

Jarrod, my friend, and the person who changed my perspective on good and evil.

...and finally, all the men and women in the fields of spiritual, religious, philosophical and metaphysical teaching from whom I have learned much, and who are many of the Giants after whom this book is titled.

INTRODUCTION
▼

About this Book

What you are about to read is the record of a personal search for spiritual answers: A mental quest for a solution I could accept as my own but would satisfactorily explain, adopt, and work alongside the religions and metaphysical teachings I have studied and respected over many years. This book is made up of a series of internal dialogues in the form of questions and answers that took place over a two year period. They were with what I can best describe as my Inner Guides. Who or what these guides are, is discussed in Chapters five and thirteen - so for the purposes of this introduction let's just say that they are the messengers within each of us who help us communicate with our higher selves - or at least beyond our everyday consciousness.

This work was originally intended just for my own use. But, as the material formed over time, I recognized that it was something I could share with others - and that's how this book came about. I will be happy if it imparts to you just some of the guidance and help it has given (and *continues* to give) me.

Complexity

Feedback from those who helped me pull this work together is that this is a complex book, especially for those who are new to the kind of concepts and teachings it offers. To help with this:

1. **Chapter Reviews:** I provide three to five statements at the end of each chapter to give an interpretation of at least a few of its main points. However, don't let these detract from anything that you may pick up on as personally significant or timely – they are intended only to help clarify and summarize what can be, especially later in the book, quite complex exchanges.

2. **Sequence of Reading:** The first time you read this book, please do so in order from first to last chapter. This is because:

   a) The dialogues in each chapter evolved over time, and some of the concepts in earlier exchanges were further developed and explained in those that came later.
   b) The complexity increases as the dialogues go on.
   c) You will see that some information was (and still is) hard for me to accept and grasp, so I often looped back on concepts, and received clarity and new insights each time.

   So, please read the book in order – You will get more from it that way.

3. **Revisiting the Book:** Everyone who has read this work, including me, re-reads Chapters (and sections within them) to gain clarity and more insight. Then, once you have been through the book fully, keep it in a convenient place and refer to it from time to time. I still do this myself, opening it at random, and each time I find new insights, interpretations and timely reminders.

Some Comments on "readiness"

There are many great books on this subject. I believe at this point in my life that all such books have come about in different styles, levels of complexity and content so that each type of reader can find something that works for him or her. For example, Judeann Glover, a kindred spirit, friend and gifted healing touch practitioner based in California who helped edit this work, put it perfectly when she observed: "You don't have to agree with – or even 'get' everything offered in this (or any) book to find bits and pieces that add to what you feel is your personal truth or the collage of your spirituality. We are really *creating* our perspective – one insight at a time."
And so it is my sincere hope that this book connects some dots and provides ideas for those creating their own spiritual pathway. If you read it, and it makes sense in whole or part, I believe your view on the world and your purpose in it will be different in some way. If that happens, even to a small degree, then this book will have served its purpose. If it makes no sense at all or you disagree with it, put it away for a while and try another source. Maybe you'll come back to this book later. It is a patient friend, and will wait for you.

The Personal Pronoun for God

Throughout this book I use the male personal pronoun to reference God in the third person. This is not intended as a suggestion that God is a human or animate male (this will become very clear in the text) but just to keep things simple. If you need to, please substitute the given pronoun with whatever you prefer.

CHAPTER 1

▼

Why am I searching for purpose and spiritual guidance now, with all the responsibilities I have with my career and providing for my family?

You have spent your life being very busy. You have been committed to the material world, and held an underlying belief that risk of failure is high and material loss is imminent. You have also connected the loss of material things with failure, embarrassment, and betrayal - even by those you have felt obliged to materially and morally support.

Well, I do have responsibility for my family!

That sense of responsibility is a function of society and how it maintains itself, based on control through sense of duty and responsibility. In reality, your *purpose* is not to support others. We will talk about your purpose, later. You need to support yourself, and your family needs to support themselves - you are one of their resources. If you were to become unable to support them, or go away, then they would find another way.

That makes me feel disposable.

So perhaps this is more about your need to be needed, than their need for you.

Ouch… maybe.

It does not matter. What you need to realize is that you can let go of your self-restricting sense of responsibility for them, and see that the way you can help them best is to empower them so they *don't* need you. As well, what you should seek to give them is your love. Also, you can be a two-way mirror through which you observe them and in which they can see themselves. This will become clearer later. Now, what has your past experience been in how others take care of <u>you</u>?

My experience has been that I have got burdened and betrayed!

Consider that your past experience is only a remembered, singular perspective of events that others did not perceive the same way you did. Negative experiences such as those you consider betrayals were necessary to show you that you can survive and that you did not really need what (or who) you lost. This goes for both things and relationships. You truly need nothing from the material world in which you are involved. Realizing this is a critical step in the evolution of your true identity.

That's easy to say - But as I said, I've been hurt many times now, and that makes me angry.

It's understandable that you are angered by the memory of the apparent betrayals you have endured. And *apparent* is a deliberate choice of words here. Now it's time to see that these events were inevitable steps in your evolution – they could even be considered gifts.

Oh come now – I can't bring myself to see a betrayal as a gift.

Each event, even a negative one, plays a part in setting you free in a way that you cannot do for yourself. Sometimes, you don't take opportunities to move on when you need to… and therefore you receive the 'push' you need.

That sounds like rough treatment - why would I need or deserve to be pushed?

Because your conscious mind and ego are sometimes lagging your spirit's intent and mission. The universe (for want of a better name at this time) does nothing to hurt you, but provides events that your spirit requires, even if your mind and ego think differently.

Will I continue to get these "pushes"?

Now that you are becoming more aware, the painful breaks apparently created against your will are going to be less frequent or jarring.

OK. So, for example, the time I had to leave a job early that paid really well – was that one of these "pushes"?

That was a well paid job at which you were very unhappy! Consider this: Did you not sense your own role in making that break with an environment which was great materially but spiritually barren?

Yes - I know what you mean - I needed to get out. But I could not bring myself to give up the income!

And so you subconsciously showed yourself the exit. But, once done, again you blamed others... because you wanted to see yourself as a victim: To project your sense of guilt. But you are now seeing that you knew what was required - and took action, even if subconsciously. In time, you will make such decisions with greater ease, faster, and with confidence and self-responsibility. And you will no longer need to delay or blame others.

But look what happened! I lost income as a result!

Think about it; you made good use of the time. That time was necessary for you to learn enough to 'move on'. You made the time to receive and seek the information you needed to increase your spiritual awareness and receptivity. Such a break is given to many, but few use it fully.

OK, but now I have read so much by the masters and gurus, I don't know which way to go next!

You have been worried about which source is right, and whether you are getting false guidance. But you are beginning to see that the various guides/teachings that you thought were very different are actually similar in their core messages. This recognition of the similarities and even convergence of ideas will increase for you over time. In the meantime, differences in teachings do <u>not</u> make some or all of them wrong, but are just the inevitable result of:

- Differing styles and perspectives of the teachers
- The loss in translation that any use of words creates
- Confusion that happens to any attempt to understand eternal truths with human logic (in fact it's not possible, as we will find out)
- The fact you are also reading them through your own perspective 'lens', which further complicates things.

Indeed, any other reader of the words in this book will make their own translation of them.

So what do I do or choose?

Don't DO or choose anything. Don't look for the differences, but rather see the *commonalties*. Don't expect perfection in any one teacher – they are "only human" as you might say. Follow their guidance (or not) via your sense of what feels right, not evidence or logic. Remember this: *Judge none of them. Listen to all of them.*

I'm still not sure why I am doing all this now, at this time.

Timing is everything... Not human time, but rather *experience* time. In fact, "experience volume" is a better way to see it than "time". You have participated in enough experiences in the world to break away from your complete immersion in it. This is deliberate, however. To be where you are now, spiritually, you must have experienced total belief in the world into which you were born.

Again - why NOW?

Because what you currently consider "God" desires your awareness back for something. And you don't have to be dead to do that since you are never really alive in the sense of separateness from Him. But He (and therefore you) has something that requires you to be connected to Him again and not fully tied up in this particular dream. This is not an emergency; it's something He (and you) planned.

I'm confused. What do you mean He wants my awareness back?

To help you understand, remember your friend RC's comment about the Holy Spirit and its "hook"? He often says that "once the hook is in you, you cannot get free". This is true in that once you begin to be aware of the Truth, then you will always be aware of it (although you can choose to ignore it, you're only fooling yourself). The difference is not that there is a hook in you as such (for God to reel you in like a fish!) but that you have a kind of leash that you run to the end of with an "ouch" several times in your life. At those moments you know about the leash... and start to ask questions.

So here I am, then. I have a lot of questions.

Review

1. Negative experiences show you that you can survive, and if they involve loss, they help you see that you no longer need what (or who) you lost.

2. Each loss you experience sets you free in a way that you cannot (or refuse to) do for yourself.

3. When studying spiritual and religious sources, don't look for the differences, but see the commonalties. Adopt those that feel right, not just those that seem logical or proven. "Judge none of them; Listen to all of them".

CHAPTER 2

—————▼—————

What Now? Where do I go from here?

There is much to tell. You should continue to seek ways to hear us - there are many. And we guide you constantly. You are beginning to see this. Do not think that we provide instructions on mundane things – this is just you seeking approval or being lazy. We provide clear signposts on events of broader significance to your desired experience.

Does that mean I have to be a fatalist?

No. You choose each event in your life - *in the current instant*. At that instant, the different possibilities also manifest which you *could* experience. Our role is to be here for you when you become aware of what the world really is. The purpose of human life is to provide a stage on which all physical experiences can be observed relative to your true self – which is a part of God. Without such experience, you are unable to see your human self *in relation* to your true self. Once you are aware of the truth, Human experience also enables you to measure your evolutionary spiritual progress. Once you've reached a certain level of awareness, we are here to guide you in your next step. That is where you are, now.

Has my life up until this point been a waste of time, then?

Here is something which is very important for you to understand and to be able to see the truth: *Time does not exist. There is only now*. So, time is never really wasted. Your life up to this point never really happened in terms of time past - since there is only now. But you have had the experience, believed it, and it seems to have been very real. The concept of time is required in the worldly experience for you to make sense of progress and cause and effect.

That's hard to grasp. My life so far does seem to have been very real – it's all I know, in fact.

You have to believe the worldly experience happened in terms of past human time for that experience to be valid and not just an idea or theory. This is required to create the stage we just described. In reality, however, you only exist in the now, and whatever you're about to do, at any time, may not have anything to do with what you thought you would be doing. Your human world will be what you choose it to be at that moment. So, there is only the now, and you're getting what you need out of it in "real-time".

This is very complicated.

Think of God's creation ["omniverse[1]" is a better description of what was being referred to here] as a mesh of potentialities. There are an infinite number of them yet you (Simon) are humanly aware of only one of them at a time – in your case the one your Soul has chosen for you to see and experience. Simultaneously then, there are many other potentialities or "what ifs" in the mesh, all of which can occur, and all of which your Soul can choose to experience.

But it's all happening together, right?

Your Soul experiences the potentialities it chooses all at the same time, but, while experiencing them as a human manifestation of your Soul, you (Simon) believe that there is only the one you are in,

---

1 If the term "universe" refers to the entirety of our human reality, Omni- is a prefix meaning "all", making the omniverse encompass all possible universes.

and it is taking real, passing, irreversible time to do it. At the Soul level, there is no time limit on how long your Soul has to experience all the possibilities in the mesh.

What about so called "past" lives, then?

Past lives are a level of the mesh. Again, they do not occur in a past time, they are all experiences your Soul can and is having in this moment. Each potentiality includes the birth and death of the personas through which the Soul experiences it. Think of it this way: Imagine you have home movie recordings of your lives which are filmed at the same time they are viewed and that you can play and swap out these movies whenever you want and no time goes by as you do this. Instead of the time passing, what changes is the volume (amount) of the experience you have had in creating and watching the movie. When your Soul is satisfied (which means that it has experienced all that it desired to experience), it can return to God.

How long does this take?

The short answer is no time at all – there is no time, remember? But each human life feels as long as you live it. In reality, the [instantaneous] process is complete when you have acquired all you wanted from your human experience. And remember that there is no such thing as time - so actually, everyone becomes enlightened at the same moment..., which is also now.
If you can let go of time, much of this will be easier to understand...
It's the human tendency to think of everything in terms of scarcity,
especially with time, that makes this hard to understand.

I'm trying – go on...

Remember that everyone's human lives in the mesh are all done in an instant. That's confusing if you are still thinking in terms of time as you have known it. In truth, your world, all this apparent activity, takes no time. No time is used, since it does not exist. Only experience is <u>created</u>, and this is God.

OK. So what do I do now?

Try to stop thinking about doing things within time. Continue to learn and prepare yourself, and be clear about what you desire to progress spiritually. Envision and seek to manifest only that – not worldly infrastructure. Get clear about what you desire spiritually, and the universe will provide the material means and events to make that happen.

Review

1. The purpose of the world is to provide a stage on which you can observe physical experiences relative to yourself and the highest version of yourself you can imagine.

2. Time does not exist; there is only the current moment. But a façade of time is required in the *human experience* for you to make sense of progress and cause and effect.

3. The omniverse is a "mesh" of all the possible events and things (potentialities) that could occur. There are an infinite number of possibilities, but you are humanly aware of only one of them at a time - the one you have chosen to see and experience in your current life. Others play out simultaneously, but you are not (usually) aware of them.

CHAPTER 3

───────▼───────

I seem to have got nowhere in the last few weeks with all this. What's happened? Am I stalled?

Don't be in such a hurry. You do not have to learn anything in order to progress now. Anything you read or study serves only to help you *accept* what you know, not *increase* what you know.

No, I mean I am not *progressing.*

Why do you say that? People in your life are telling you about how much you are changing and learning, are they not? And you have become more and more aware of yourself, and what you are. Progressing, you are!

OK Yoda, so how do I work out what to do next?

As per the previous discussion, it is not a matter of you planning what to do, but being clear about what you desire.

How can I know what I desire when I don't know what to do?

That's an interesting question - and one which reflects how you are 'back to front' with your life. You seem to be so interested in <u>doing</u> before you know what you desire… You've lived a lot of your life that way: Doing things and assuming you'll find out what you really desire as you go along, or perhaps when you finish. Now, at this moment in your life, you have to pause and work out what you truly desire, and then you'll see what, if anything, you need to *do*.

I have to work out what I want to be, first, then?

Yes. It's not what you want to DO, but what you want to BE. And that does not mean you want to be a butcher, a baker or candlestick maker. It means what do you want to be while you're doing worldly things and what you want to be to others and yourself? What do you want to <u>accept</u>, rather than do?

I'm struggling with that.

How do you want to be able to respond to the world? Are you willing to observe it rather than control it?

Do you mean that I don't have to do anything specifically?

Yes and no. Follow through on the things you want to know more about; that will give you the confidence to do new things and accept what is. Follow through on what interests you. Practice it. Become confident with it in terms of others' expectations so you can share it with them, confidently. But try things without expectation or anticipation. Be passionate about the experience, and not vested in the end result. Be open to what comes along.

OK. Let's change the subject a bit. I am feeling guilty about not working and earning with every moment I have. Should I?

Welcome to abundance. There are no dire consequences to you sitting doing what you are doing right now, in this moment. There is no judgment, or right and wrong[2]. There just is. You can rest easy, having done all that has been asked of you. Do not question whether or not it was good enough. You 'did your best', and that is always good enough, just as Ruiz says in his book *The Four*

---

2 Note this statement - This becomes a fundamental point in these dialogues.

Agreements (see Recommended Reading). In fact, let's revisit his other three Agreements and use them to help you:

1. Be Impeccable With Your Word. You know that as your ego takes over, you verbalize it, and as you do so, the act strengthens the ego's grip on you. Accept it when it happens - and over time seek to recognize its arousal earlier and earlier and *decline* participation in it. As it rises, deliberately verbalize something else. Perhaps "let it be". There is no coincidence that these moments happen at certain times – for example when you are stuck in traffic or watching the news on television. But each of those environments provides fuel for the awakening of the ego and Eckhart Tolle's "pain body"[3] in you: You're surrounded by angry people in traffic, or watching newscasts about what you see as a hypocritical and often diabolical world. It's very simple: When you are alone and quiet, especially taking-in enlightened messages on CDs or in books, it's easier to stay at a higher level. You can *refresh* yourself in these moments, but you must apply what you have learned and *hone* yourself during the necessary interaction with the world: That is its purpose.

2. Don't Take Anything Personally. You have a saying: "Everyone is <u>you</u> living <u>their</u> way". Well, if you believe that (and you should), then no-one really intends you harm - unless they are not spiritually conscious, in which case they are trapped within a shell, and their lives have programmed them to treat their <u>perception</u> of you a certain way. It is their shell that treats you poorly or indifferently, not them. And you would do exactly the same if you were trapped inside their shell. Their shell is treating your shell in a certain way. It's nothing to do with the real you or the real them. Observe it, understand them, and forgive yourself.

3. Don't Make Assumptions. You spend a lot of time making assumptions about what you should be doing [in your career], worrying what your client thinks you are doing, and how they think you're performing. But none of it effects the moment of now, and most of it is a wrong assumption anyway. So, follow Ruiz's advice

---

3 Tolle (2006) describes the "pain body" is the result of years of conditioned thought patterns, individually and collectively, which accumulate within us and form a personality of their own. During 'pain-body attacks' we respond from the agenda of this entity.

– Do your best and don't assume that it's not enough or will come to naught. Do it, and let it be. In fact, live that way. Do it, and let it be.

"Let it be". So that's a good approach, right?

Yes. We know you try to describe annoying events or situations in a way so as to avoid using them to create victim status for yourself. You can simplify this using "Let it be". For example, instead of steadying your mind by saying "His car is there and mine is here" when someone cuts you off on the highway, try simply saying "let it be". Spend <u>no</u> energy and thought, but allow your new acceptance to occur smoothly and swiftly without justification or analysis. Recognize the negative reaction and let it go - accept peace sooner and without effort.

That seems to be an overall piece of advice for me.

Indeed. Accept each moment, let it be. If you use Ruiz's *Four Agreements* then the future will be defined by the rightness of now, and you will have chosen the results accordingly. So you can trust that there will be nothing to fear. Let it be.

Oh dear - I'm not sure I have lived that well!

Guess what? Let it be. A Christian may tell you you're a sinner and God accepts that you are not perfect.   Now, while you are not a sinner in terms of being destined for hell (there is no hell as such and we'll talk about that later), you are getting better and better – but for yourself... not for God, or for anyone else. You know it, and will know what that means as the next moment unfolds. Simply work patiently and peacefully to follow what you are learning and accept where you are, and what happens. In the new space that doing this will open to you, look for our signs and follow your intuition to something wholly new.

If I am to follow what the gurus like Ruiz tell me, which guru is the best?

They are all right in their own way. They differ only in their interpretation of the truth and their human programming, as well as written and spoken language limitations. From each of them, take the signposts that mean something to you at this moment. Hear and accept them from beyond human logic and critical thinking. Then, know that imperfections and contradictions are and will always be part of *your own* teachings. Do not be afraid to give your own teachings anyway, but do not defend them - for that means resistance and ceasing progress. Be not afraid to change your mind once your experience shows you more and more of the Truth. Your understanding will change – we will not show you everything at once. You will see this in these dialogues. And everything will change, when you are ready.

Review

1. Be involved and excited about your life desires and experiences, but don't get hung up on the end result.

2. When you feel frustration or annoyance, "let it be". Spend no energy and thought, but allow acceptance to occur smoothly and quickly without justifying or analyzing it: Accept reality and peace as soon as you can.

3. Don't be afraid to change your mind when you have learned something new, especially if at first it caused you discomfort or annoyance.

CHAPTER 4

—————▼—————

It's been a bad couple of weeks for business. What am I doing wrong?

You have opted out of the game. But you have opted out without being able to be truly *free* of it. That's why you feel scared. Although you say you have, you have not accepted this world is not really what it appears to be and that you are more than what you thought; and thus, as the world becomes more and more 'real', the worse it gets, and that's how the ego keeps control of you. And so your ego is creating the pain deliberately to make the world seem more real and thus create a need for its existence – to protect you. Are you feeling like you may not be able to provide for your family?

Yes, that's right.

Then your ego has taken over. Gently push it into the background now. Stop feeling sorry for yourself and don't let fear make your decisions for you. Why would you give everything up so easily, Simon? And why do you continue to think someone will rescue you, will say "yes you're right - you do deserve better, the world has been unfair and I'll spank it for you"? You sound just like your son, crying "It's not fair Daddy!"

OK, OK. Ouch.

Are words such as those necessary to snap you out of this?

Maybe.

Get out of self pity and back to your journey. What do you want to do next? Why not try a few things out? Not to make a lot of money or even a long term thing, but just to see what it's like? Life's purpose is to try things out - what's the cost of failure here? Really?

I'm lazy I guess.

Apathetic, maybe. But, it's because you're afraid – afraid of failure. Beat the fear, and you'll beat the apathy. Now, what happens if you don't get that high paying job, and you run out of savings?

I would have to sell up – move home and all. So I am thinking I should be proactive in downsizing our lives.

As you keep saying (be careful about that!) one bad break and the savings are gone in an instant, anyway. And how happy will you be looking back on how quickly you gave in? You know what you are doing this time: Thinking about failure, telling other people (in the hope they can fix something for you) and all the while these thoughts of yours and others is <u>making</u> the bad option happen. This time, you KNOW that. That's the difference. So, now you have to break out of the fog and the fear and create something positive.

But I want to provide for my family!

Get out of the victim mode. Remember your family is not separate from you, nor are they your sole responsibility in the broader sense. That's what your ego wants you to believe. You will serve your family best by being there for them, providing wisdom and serenity, and letting them go when it's time. And those things don't take money - They take attention and love, neither of which you can give if you're unhappy and feeling sorry for yourself.

What do I do, then?

Focus on and create what you DO desire, instead of what you don't. Stop dwelling on the risks, and the fear, and the dire possibilities. Wake up tomorrow ready to work out how to make it work, not how to throw in the towel. If you only had a month to live - would you still consider the need to give everything up?

OK. I get it.

Review

1. Avoid the trap of seeing yourself as a 'victim'.

2. Trust that you are only truly responsible for <u>yourself</u>.

3. Think positively: Focus on and create what you DO desire, instead of what you don't.

CHAPTER 5

———————▼———————

I think these 'conversations' are really with me, myself. And if I don't already know about something then I won't get an answer from you. Right?

Let's start this way - Who do you think we are?

You're my collected thoughts and subconscious conclusions; data and ideas stashed away that don't come out during normal thinking processes.

You're right. And we are more, too. There is nothing you do not know that you need to know - or put another way, you already know everything you need.

How about if I ask about something about which I know nothing? Will you be able to answer questions about that? For example, my friend RC requested me to ask you about the titanium ore brought ashore by the Tsunami in Southern Asia and India a while back - why did that happen?

Why would we tell you something which you, Simon, have no real desire to know or need to understand? That would be without purpose.

That's a cop-out! If you're something bigger than me, then you'll know all the answers.

We will give you an answer which is relevant to your state of readiness and seeking as follows: We don't know what you and the collective consciousness of the world will choose, nor will we tell you what to do. We only give support and direction. We know all the possible human outcomes (we have seen the mesh of them all), but not the choices you will make individually or collectively at this moment which defines which potentiality/outcome you will follow with this particular life.

Hold on. Back to the point - I made no choices about the Tsunami.

Maybe not. But after it happened, did you wish for the area to recover in some way - hope that something good came out of the event?

Yes. Of course I did.

Did many others?

Yes... millions of right-minded people. In fact, I believe efforts were made by large numbers of new-age-minded people to focus their collective intent and energy on the crisis in order to help people there. I believe this action has been credited for a low level of disease outbreaks after the disaster.

What else did people desire for the region? Were they specific and unified in their vision of help?

I don't know – but I am sure they hoped the region would recover materially and financially etc.

Then see the Titanium as a miraculous manifestation of the vague good wishes of millions.

Come now - what will the people there really be able to do with ten feet high deposits of titanium ore left on sand dunes a mile inshore?

That's up to them, and for those who can help them. The universe provided something from those general wishes for economic recovery for the region.

That's a bit of a weak and vague explanation, frankly.

But, does it answer your question to the level with which you personally have any real care or interest?

Yes, but would you answer my friend RC differently?

We would answer his real question if he were willing to ask it and hear the answer. But what about your underlying question here – which is why we cannot tell you things about which you know nothing?

Yes, what about that?

Do you think that would help you, now, if we drove a million facts and figures into your head?

Well it might save me a lot of reading and be proof of your superiority!

There are many reasons we will not do this. The main reason is that for anything to have meaning requires a relative opposite by which it can be observed. Pure data creates no understanding. It needs to be seen in context - in relationship to other things so that it can make sense. That is why computers do not 'think' like you do. For you to be able to see and understand anything, it has to be a) In the context of your life up to this point and b) Be appropriate to your readiness to receive it. You receive data exactly when you need it to evolve your choices. If we gave you data that was outside this, it would be useless to you... like teaching algebra to a baby.

You mean I'd fail the comprehension test after the lesson?

You could put it like that. This is also why spiritual messages are many and varied - each of them are delivered to people in the countless states of contextual and spiritual readiness in which humanity exists.

But wait. If you were to make me know lots of information that would show me you're something really special... really larger than me.

Oh - You want a personal miracle; a show of power? We provide only insights that are appropriate to your experience. But that said Simon, *would you be satisfied if you somehow knew some amazing things that you have not learned in the usual way? They simply were there, in your head, in a manner in which you could hear and understand them?*

Yes! That's exactly what I am saying! Can you do that?

Thy will be done.

Really?

I am laughing. Do you not see that these works, these dialogues, these answers, are and will be, just that?[4]

---

4 Many months after this dialogue, I read a book by Jane Roberts in which she talked with a skeptical psychologist who was seeking proof that there was more to life than cause and effect - by finding someone who could tell him things no-one else could know. She answered him with this question: "Why not catch yourself with knowledge you're not supposed to have?" (Roberts, The Magical Approach, 1995, p. 147)

Review

1. Pure data, knowledge or information creates no understanding, no wisdom.

2. For you to be able to understand and make use of anything, it has to be relative to the context of your life at that point; the stage in the journey of your life. Everything else is just noise.

3. At moments of important life choices, you will receive the information you need - if you are open to it.

CHAPTER 6

─────────▼─────────

I bought two books to help me work out what I want to be[5]. I went through them and completed the exercises they provided. I think I'm getting clearer that there's nothing I can DO in order to BE what I want. If I work out what I want to BE, then the DO will happen on its own.

OK.

I think I'm picking up that it's more complex than that...

Yes. But that does not matter. What matters is what *you* are ready for, *now*.

OK. Before, when you said I should work out what I *do desire,* not what I *don't desire*, I kept slipping back to doing things. But you advised that I need to work out what I want to BE, at a deeper level. And that does not mean a career or job or a business, but 'being' in terms of a true purpose.

In the same way as Neale Donald Walsh says in *Conversations with God,* you cannot have what you "want" (the act of wanting defines and creates the lack itself), you cannot DO what you want to BE (the act of struggling to DO something defines and creates the lack

─────────

5 *Recreating Yourself* and *Bringers of the Light* by Neale Donald Walsch - details provided in Recommended Reading.

of that, too). In your case, you <u>want</u> a great job or contract and are DOING lots of things to make that happen. But just as you have to first know what thing you desire and then *believe* you have it, you have to first know what you seek to BE and then believe you ARE that - and then the things of your truly desired DOING (be that a job, career, business or whatever) will manifest.

Wow! I think I get that. It's completely the opposite of what we do with our lives though, right?

Yes. Now, what did you discover from the books?

I want to BE five things:

- **Healthy**
- **Positive**
- **Patient**
- **Open-minded**
- **Guiding**

Have you started?

Yes. I wrote down what I did to <u>be</u> each of these, today, and compared that to what I was doing before - and it was clear that what I did before was <u>not</u> enabling me to be what I want to be!

Good. It will take a while to break old habits. But you have already found that once you are ready, you can do what seemed impossible, just moments before. You did it for quitting smoking and now diet and exercise – you lost 20lb in 2 months. Changes can be dramatic or simple - you just have to be ready.

That's excellent - and very encouraging actually!

Do you have any other questions for us?

Yes. Do you speak to me through other people, like my wife, Alice?

Why?

Today, Alice and I went out for lunch. We were in a restaurant looking out the window at a sunny day, talking about whether I should be looking for a job back in the corporate world or continuing consulting. I was sure (and feeling pressured that) she really wanted me to be back in a full time work. But then out of nowhere she announced that it was a great thing I wasn't because I used the time flexibility to get myself in physical shape - which was actually much more important right now for her and the family! It was so *obvious* and so right and so freeing from the stress I have been putting myself under.

Does it matter if it's someone or something else talking to you? The fact is we are all one, each of us a mouthpiece and a source of guidance for each other. Attribute wisdom not to the speaker, but to your *remembrance* (i.e. you already knew it) of what they said. Since all of us know the same thing – Every*thing we need to know, now.*

Actually, it's another aspect of the perspective that everyone is me, living their way: Whatever anyone does or says is really to them - and that's me.

Another important thing about what Alice said to you - Remember that having a new or better job or contract is not truly what you want to BE – it's a situation, not a state of being. As you have demonstrated, you truly desire to be healthy – and it's that which has manifested. Such progress in one day!

Ah. One day. Time. That's a bother for me. I feel guilty for spending all this time on this work with you and the books etc. I feel I should be working on something more tangible.

You mean something worldlier and revenue-generating, right? Hopefully, our discussion here has helped that. Overall though, remember that you're in the process of 'remembering' that your purpose here is **not** to remain stuck in the games of the human experience. If you were to die tomorrow, you would have achieved more in this life by what you discovered *in writing this chapter* than you would by working 24/7 and earning millions of dollars until you were a hundred years old. Learn to BE... and the rest, if it matters, will happen along the way.

OK. I feel better seeing it that way.

Review

1. You fail to get or do things that you *want* because the act of wanting only creates greater want.

2. You have to first know what you seek to BE and then believe you already ARE that. Then your truly desired DOING (be that a job, career, business or whatever) will come about.

3. Know that when you see wisdom in others, it is actually your own. The speaker just helped you remember – think of it this way: Every 'a-ha' is a déjà-vu.

CHAPTER 7

━━━━━━━▼━━━━━━━

I'd like to be wealthier. I'm happy with what I have, but would like more - even if it were only for security.

The result of what you are seeking in your recent efforts is spiritual growth itself, not any worldly material resulting from it: And so it should be - Worldly material is not lasting. This is important for you to know. Deep and real spiritual growth will require and create in you a recognition of the abundance you have, right <u>now</u>, along with a steady reduction in the need for (and interest in) material things - which become increasingly irrelevant. When this happens, you are deciding and demonstrating that you are and will always be more than worldly "stuff".

But I could have so much more worldly comfort and more cool things...

Yes. But do you *desire* it? *Truly desire* it? Or is it just *wanting...* from jealousy, or fear, or doing what others expect or are doing?

Maybe, but what if I end up penniless and on the street?

Do you want that to happen?

No!

Then it won't, not if you really desire something else, genuinely, at the deepest level. As we have said, *it's about knowing what you do desire, not thinking about what you want to avoid*. Listen – this is absolutely essential for you to understand, so that you can change your way of thinking: *Don't think about not wanting disaster, but instead think about the positive alternative... Think about health and wealth and happiness and not avoidance of illness, poverty or sorrow.*

That's easy to say but it's the way I think – and other people too, I believe!

Yes. Just as a child crushes his favorite toy in a fit of frustration, you are capable of creating through attraction and *doing* (i.e. you have free will) things in this world that are not what you truly desire or want to *be*. And all the while you are missing out on the abundance of now... for fear of not having it later. But, there is no later, only now. For example: Give a homeless man a good meal, and at that moment, he is more satisfied and has a higher level of fulfillment than the rich man, bored and alone in his mansion. Indeed, here's a concept which is very alien to the usual mindset of people - The closer you are to having and wanting nothing, the more you can live in the moment, the now, and thus the more you truly have. Because when the now is your only (or most loved) possession, since the now is all there is, you have *everything*.

Can't I have the now <u>and</u> some more wealth?

Yes, but know that material wealth gets in the way of the now - as you first spend all your effort getting it, then even more effort keeping it. It is not necessary, and not real. As Jesus said, "It is easier for the camel to pass through the eye of a needle than for a rich man to enter the Kingdom of God." Just as the traders had to unload the camel to get through the gate, so must you offload what you carry.

But cool stuff can make for a great moment of now!

If you consider being lost in a moment through complete absorption in an illusion, then that is true. But true awareness of the moment itself, the bliss of oneness with God, cannot be compared.

Perhaps I am more worried about losing everything - that's happened to others. I don't want that!

So to prevent losing what you have, you want more? That's an interesting conclusion. As for those other people not wanting to lose the material things they had: Are you sure they did not want that? Sure, what you see and what society would tell you is they were "destroyed" by loss, and their mind and ego probably indeed did not want to lose their stuff. But are you willing to consider that loss is what their Soul chose to experience? Tell me, Simon, to lose your money - is that really to lose EVERYTHING? Are material comforts all you really are?

Well I'm sure those people felt like they lost everything!

Do you think that you'd be left to starve to death if material things changed? Did you not start again materially after you split from your first long-term relationship and then again when you split from your first wife? Did you not suddenly find yourself living in a foreign country with no money, a house in England worth less than the mortgage and no job? And did you shrivel up and die?

Well, I guess not.

You dealt with it because you knew what you desired and believed. You had a vision of what life would be like on the other side of the grief and believed it was there and you desired it fully. And just as importantly, you didn't *disbelieve* in the OK-ness of your future. Active disbelief in abundance is worse than just not believing - since it creates the opposite of what you desire, not just a lack of it.
So, now, focus on what <u>you</u> are becoming, and let others find their own way. And yes, you should help those less fortunate - the

homeless, starving, sick. But you cannot take their true journey for them.

I see. I have already succeeded in recovering from loss - several times. I just keep forgetting that.

Yes, repeatedly. You're good at forgetting.

OK. Point made. Now I have a related question. The abundance theories say I should give thanks for already having what I desire - but that just feels silly when I clearly don't have it.

Think about what you just said - You do already have what you truly desire! Look around you. And you've been happy with it. What you mean is you now think that you desire more. But do you, really?

I think so.

Well that's not enough. If you don't *really* desire something, then you won't manifest it. In the meantime, accept and <u>give thanks</u> for that which you do have.

Wait - maybe it's more like what I said... about wanting security.

Let me repeat what I said above - You are missing out on the abundance of now... for fear of not having it later. But, there is no later, only now.

But my friend RC said he wants more and I assume he means it. He asked me the questions above about how silly it seems to give thanks for something we clearly don't possess yet. Can you give guidance on that?

Until recently neither of you needed any more than you already have. That was abundance to you, and from that perspective, you can indeed thank God for having everything you need. Some people have all the stuff they desire because they believe they have it and deserve it, totally. And it is so. Some people desire and need more stuff than others. Think about it. Each time you have truly desired something, did you get it? I mean truly desired it, thought about it, imagined having it with a belief that somehow it would be yours?

Well, yes I suppose so. Except a few ladies I adored from afar!

First, people are not objects. You cannot manifest their experiences for them. Second, if you'd like some more 'stuff', then don't thank God for what you don't have - that would indeed be delusional thinking. Instead, continue to thank Him for what you DO have and your gift of the <u>potential</u> for more and your plans to get it - IF you truly desire it. Then once you know what you truly desire, try out the various ways to tap the laws of attraction, while still thanking God for what you have, along with what you believe is coming. When the new stuff comes along, you are simply thanking God for what you truly have, at that moment. And there's no delusion in that. Give thanks for the *potential,* your God given powers, as well as the *manifested.*

I guess I do know that some people who have all the stuff they desire are not happy.

Those who are wealthy yet desire spiritual wealth feel an underlying sense of lack no matter what material possessions they accumulate. Other people can achieve complete fulfillment from material things, but usually only for a part of their lives. And that is their choice.

Review

1. Spiritual growth creates recognition of the abundance you have in <u>this</u> moment, and a reduction in appetite for material things.

2. The less you want and expect (which tend to be future focused), the more you can live in the moment. It makes sense therefore that when you can live only in the moment (the now), if now is all there is, you have everything.

3. Material wealth gets in the way of the now - you first spend all your effort and awareness to get it, then even more to keep it (both of which are future, not now- focused).

4. "It's not having what you want, it's wanting what you've got" (from the song *Soak Up The Sun* by Sheryl Crow/Jeff Trott)

CHAPTER 8

▼

I read an article describing the tortures of prisoners of the Iraqi regime of Saddam Hussein, and an email exchange between people arguing about whether the Americans torture Iraqi POWs. It made me feel angry and repulsed to see what was done - and to see the email argument, too! It seems that the email debaters are more concerned about who is doing it (and can be blamed) in terms of governments or religions than what is actually happening between the people involved.

It is at the individual level that all of this matters. Assignment of blame to organizations is an excuse not to look at the truth – that it's *people* who do this to each other.

I understand that, but regardless, I find it so hard to believe in the goodness of God when I see such images. I want to step in because God apparently will not!

Based on our knowledge of who you want to be, the next higher version of yourself, you should not intervene.

What? How can I <u>not</u> step in and stop such horrors, and punish the perpetrators?

The cruelty that one man perpetrates on another is between the two of them, "the Players", for each of them participates willingly, their subconscious always knowing of their complicity and the fleetingness of their misery compared to the myriad of human (and other) lives in the mesh of potentialities. An observer, full of anger at the injustice that he sees, has no superiority and responsibility to end the game. Rather, he should allow it to play out, and be ready to help both players in their aftermath.

Allow it? How can that be?

Without such an observer, how can the wicked prove and measure their wickedness, or the victims prove and measure their tragedy? And how can these events be seen relative to, and therefore make necessary, love and goodness? You see, it's the observer who provides the relativity and sees the experience - *on behalf of God*.

Surely God can see this and everything, Himself? He does not need us to see it!

God does not exist in this dimension, but experiences it through the eyes of those who do. That is the purpose of the world, and you - for God to experience Himself, through you.

God is looking through _my_ eyes?

By observing[6], the Observer allows the process to take its course, and plays a key role in providing the perspective that gives relativity to the horror, and by which the participants can recognize what they truly are.

So let me get this straight: The Observers, the people who witness these things occurring, are a) creating the relativity required for the victim and perpetrator, the "players" as you call them, to experience their states relative to God, and b) enabling God to

---

6 Another term for observing is "witnessing": "Clarity and peace come through what Plato, Hegel and Gurdjieff all called "witnessing"...the ability to see without getting caught up in the soap opera. ...The capacity to witness frees us." (Mundy, Awaken to Your Own Call, 1994, p. 138)

observe this world and thus experience himself by experiencing what he is not?

Observers are the perspective providing relativity within the world dimension and also are giving themselves the opportunity to experience "being God" in relation to worldly behavior. But, usually, the human Observer gets selfish and turns the players' actions into fears and nightmares that this might be his own potential future. And so he spoils his own peace, casting it aside by turning his fear into hatred and bigotry and false bravado. Or to end the Players' suffering he rides in as a hero, a savior, only to create the very death and destruction that he claims to be against. And in all these, the Observer actually fails the players before him.

You mean to help a victim and to punish a tyrant is a *failure*?

To the Observers I say this: Watch these games. Know that your sole (or *Soul*) task is to observe these poor wretches without judgment or anger - but *unflinching love*. For in doing so, you can see and experience what you truly are, while the players can play out their story and thus know what *they* truly are, by *doing what they are not...* in the observing presence of your impartiality and love. So it will be when you end both your belief that you know the victim's true purpose or best interest, and your condemnation of his assailant. You can never end these horrible games through judgment, participation, or worldly actions <u>of any kind</u>. Instead, you must transcend them through impartial observation, depthless love, and unending forgiveness. For then do you save your brothers, and yourself, and serve God.

So we do nothing? We just stand back and do nothing about these horrors in Iraq?

Are the struggles in Iraq part of *your* purpose as Simon Watson? Are they a part of the environment and life and times *you* have chosen to live this time around to create the physical embodiment of your higher self? Are they an essential part of the experience of being "Simon Watson"?

Well, no - I don't ever want to be involved in such things, but that's not the point. I cannot just stand by and let it happen!

You are not letting it happen. It just *is* happening, and is the will of the participants and the collective consciousness. If you try to stop it happening, *you have to participate in it*. And then you are choosing not to be the observer, instead re-entering the game, and in doing so, you become a player, and cease to observe. You change nothing, and relinquish the opportunity to step toward enlightenment by being as God - impartial observation, depthless love, and unending forgiveness. Simply, while playing the game with total immersion in day-to-day human experience and all its trials, Godliness is impossible.

No - that cannot be right. How could someone stand by, knowing the misery being inflicted on someone... especially if that someone is a loved one, for example?

Listen - This issue is the key to your ability to let go of this world: If you cannot let go of responsibility for others, then teach your loved ones that this world and the pains within it are but a fleeting moment that they have chosen. Teach them that they never really die; that they are God; that they are choosing their fates and even their deaths. If everyone knew this, then there would be no real suffering, even if there are a few who are not enlightened and perpetrate war.   Then, you would not have to worry about and protect your loved ones from the few moments of pain which terrify you so much - because your loved ones would not be afraid. And thus you would not have to fight on their behalf.

This requires a huge amount of blind faith; a huge change in everything!

Yes. And it is why all this madness seems to continue. But you can break the cycle, if you so choose. And remember this - all you need to do is end it for *yourself*. If you teach your loved ones what we are teaching you here, it would relieve their discomfort in the brief crises that worry you so much at this point - and thus relieve your sense of responsibility for them.

But they would not believe this! Frankly, it's hard for me to accept it and this is my own thinking!

Listen, if you accept that they cannot truly be destroyed then *your own acceptance is all that is required* to let them go, even if they do not know the truth. Beyond the human personalities and bodies you see them as, your loved ones are much stronger than you think.

Oh boy. That's going to take some thinking about.

OK.

Let me go back a step. If I understand you correctly, it is by resisting and trying to fix these things - injustice, cruelty, terror etc. that I perpetuate them and bring them into my own experience?

You have heard this many times from teachers and masters... "Turn the other cheek", "No Resistance", "What you resist persists", "What you look at, disappears" and "Give him your shirt" to give a few examples.

But I have always thought that we should fight for what is right, and fight against evil!

And that's why human existence is such a trial for so many. Stop fighting. Start observing.

But what if cruel people come along and threaten me, my family? Do I really do nothing then?

I have already answered this. But I will say more. First, don't seek to join in the fights of others - and the chances of those fights entering your life are removed. But if it is your choice to experience war in this life, perhaps by entering the wars of others, then you can choose to fight, of course. Then, war, torment and death are what you have chosen. Even then, you can choose to step out of it, just as Jesus did. He chose to die, and in the manner he did, as a demonstration of truly who he was. He observed his own torture and death from a position of forgiveness and love. "Father forgive them, for they know not what they do". You have that choice, too.

I have to admit, it's frightening to think that this is what being enlightened is all about.

I understand. God is not war or hatred or pain, but those things are part of His creation - so that peace, love and bliss might also be. Once you are ready, you will no longer be afraid of this. Your fear is based on your belief that you exist only once in this worldly experience and that one has to fight to survive for as long as possible.

OK. Supposing I can do it, I still have to defend my family! It's my job! What kind of man would I be if I did not do that?

Such macho talk only serves to keep you in the dark, even if you think it makes you look better to others. You can defend your loved ones - you can do whatever you like. You just have to choose in which way you want to help yourself. This is about you, not them.

That sounds selfish to me!

That is your ego talking, with false modesty and using the responsibilities with which you have been yoked by society. It's programming which perpetuates the illusion and traps you within it.

I have no choice but to fight if it's really necessary!

Always, there is a choice.

Not true! I'm going to use a silly example to make my point here - What if I am tied up and unable to move and cannot take an action. Then I have no choice!

We've been over this, in other ways, but it's *so* important for you to understand this point. "Choice" or "Free Will" is about what you choose to BE, not DO. Stop responding by first DOING and instead respond by BEING and let your actions and reactions come from that. You cannot achieve enlightenment by *doing* anything in this world. But what you can do, with each moment, is choose to be a higher version of yourself. Or you can be the tough fighter, the avenger. Or you can be the victim. It's your choice. Instead, Simon, why not end the cycle if only for you? Choose to see the world differently and be something else - that which you have chosen to be, the highest version of yourself, knowing the truth of how all this really works. Don't consider not fighting as weak, or meek, or pathetic. Rather, consider it as choosing *to observe yourself, in relation to the rest, from a position of peace.* And in the moments where your observations of yourself reveal a person of depthless love and unending forgiveness, then you will be closer to God. Remember: "The meek shall inherit the Earth".

Wait - you did not answer my question. I am still tied up...

OK. You are very persistent. So you're tied up and your choices are limited. But you can choose to respond to the situation in a way that suits your desired states of being (in your case, three of them are healthy, positive and patient and all three of these states suggest some actions you should and should not take while tied up!), and thus demonstrate a higher version of yourself.

I think I understand. But, assuming I'm not physically tied up for a second, I still have to DO something at moments of crisis... Even if I choose to react differently internally, what do I do externally? Do a jig, or sit on my hands? What?

Again, let go of defining your response through judgmental action or *doing*. If you respond from *being*, you will do what you are, at that moment, just as naturally as you have responded in the past. If in the past you would have lashed out, attacked, run away, acted tough, these all come from fear, immersion in doing, and possibly a desire to be something other than the things you have recently chosen to be. When you are ready, these old reactions will be replaced, quite naturally, by those that will demonstrate your chosen higher version of yourself.

But this is going to be very hard. It sounds like I have to be, well, weak.

Were Jesus, John the Baptist, Gandhi or Buddha, and all those like them, seen as such by those who knew them? Those who met them would use a very different word. Your fear of being seen as a wimp is based on how your ego thinks others in the world may interpret *your* new behavior. But when you are ready, you will no longer measure yourself by what others (or even your own ego) say, but by what you are being.

It's still a hard pill to swallow!

This transition <u>is</u> hard, Simon. Did you think that it would be easy? That you could read a book and get a certificate and wake up the next day all glowing and enlightened? As *A Course in Miracles* tells you, the ego will do everything it can to stop you! As Richard Bach's book *Illusions* showed you, enlightenment is something that will make you different - and can get you hated, feared and even killed.

I guess I didn't want to hear that. But it's too late now - I am on the journey. I am as ready as I'll ever be. What do I have to do (or rather be) now?

You have to be able to stop participating as an immersed and vested player in the game - become a true Observer.

What does that mean?

You have begun to learn how to be an *Observer,* but you slip back to being in-between... a *Spectator.* A Spectator is different to an Observer in that he tends to still get involved in the game, the spectacle, swept along by the events and vested in the result. Are you ready to be fully an Observer - fully detached and impartial?

If I was to do as you say, I would appear strange to the world! A loner, a pacifist.

Did not Jesus seem this way to many? Did not Buddha? Did not the great masters, to the point many were persecuted and even killed?

Yes, but I'm no master, no guru. They were special!

Maybe you are not a master, but you are aspiring to a new way of seeing the world and of living in it.

In *Conversations with God Book 1,* **it states that despots can be stopped - that love of self <u>and</u> the despot demands it; that sometimes man must go to war to make a statement of who he truly is. This is contradictory to what you have told me: "This should put to rest some pacifist theories that highest love requires no forceful response to what you consider evil" (Walsch,** *Conversations With God Book 1,* **1996, p. 133)**

The teaching in all books is stated through the lens of the author, the publisher, and a message designed for an audience at a certain level of readiness. Many who read *Conversations with God* find its contents shocking and too much to bear - but you did not. For you, its lessons are more a process of remembering, and as a result, some subjects need to be taken a step further for you, now. That is our purpose here. Second, if you <u>need</u> to go to war, <u>you</u> will have chosen for violence to be part of your human experience at that moment. You are not amidst the world as a helpless object, like a leaf blown about in the wind. Now, of course it is true that you're subject to the effects of collective consciousness, but remember that unless you are very different from the culture in which you exist, you will have some level of responsibility for what that collective consciousness is.

Wait a minute. Assume I am not in agreement with the collective consciousness, that I do not want to fight, but there I am, facing a despot or tyrant. Sorry, but I still think your pacifist approach is contradictory to Walsch's statements.

It is contradictory only if you ignore that we stated *you can re-enter the game at any time*. That's your choice, and to re-enter it to demonstrate the next highest version of yourself by fighting and killing in the physical world is a good use of that world.

OK. Make this simple for me. So there I am, in the middle of the situation. Which way is right - pacifist or warrior?

Statesman.

That's not a simple answer! What does that mean?

A statesman has been defined as *a person who exhibits great wisdom and ability in directing the affairs of a government or in dealing with important public issues*. So, BE a Statesman and make a decision and take action from that position, along with one which demonstrates who you want to be or who you truly are.

That's still no answer! Do I fight or not if I think there is evil that needs to be stopped?

Choices, choices, choices. Make them from a position of desiring to demonstrate your chosen state of being, and in doing so, define where you are in your journey to mastery. Think about the original *Star Wars* movie in which Obi Wan Kenobi fights Darth Vader and declares "You cannot win Darth. If you strike me down, I shall become more powerful than you can possibly imagine". Then, by his own choice, Kenobi allowed Vader to strike him, only to leave the villain kicking nervously at an empty robe rather than a dead opponent. Thus Obi Wan became a spiritual guide who helped Luke Skywalker to victory - There is much truth in that moment of cinema. Mastery is "when all possibility of hurt, damage and loss is eliminated" (Walsch, Conversations with God, 1996, p. 134). The guidance we gave you (that you call pacifism) describes <u>mastery</u>, for no master creates, enters or perpetuates harm. S/he does this by never responding with violence when war becomes an option, or by choosing for war simply not to be a possibility in his/her human existence. Masters don't need war to create and temper their being.

That makes sense in theory, but is it really practical, right now, for those people who find themselves in the situation where fighting is unavoidable?

I will say again, you always have a choice, and everyone is at different levels of readiness, and living different lives. Our advice is to YOU, not them. If you are frightened, coming from a position of fear and not love, of course you will fight instinctively. If you (or anyone) have chosen to be in a situation where you want to demonstrate who you are by fighting (and that will be against whatever you think is wrong - which is completely relative), then you can choose to fight. When you achieve mastery, you will not fight. When everyone acquires mastery, there will be no more wars.

But that's a long way off - and probably many lifetimes for a lot of Souls!

Today you, Simon, know more than you did yesterday in this matter. The question is simply this - when will you, yourself, want to use this new understanding? This is about you being *self-centered*. Be a warrior, if that's what you have chosen to be. Fight in offense or defense, if that's what you are.   It's your choice. But listen - *our guidance is about growth and change, not about perpetuation.*

Review

1. An Observer enables relativity of all the extremes that s/he sees in the world - on behalf of God; enabling the wicked to demonstrate their wickedness, and the victims to demonstrate their tragedy.   And thus is made possible the polarity of love.

   "Ultimately there are no dualities – neither black nor white, neither oppressor nor victim. We are all connected in a journey toward the happiness that is labeled enlightenment."   - His Holiness the Dalai Lama.

2. People who intervene as heroes or saviors (or allow others to use or promote them that way) only perpetuate the very angst they seek to end.

3. True Observers don't end the interactions of others. Instead, they transcend them through impartial observation, depthless love, and unending forgiveness.

4. Do not respond to attack (perceived or real) via judgmental *reaction*. Instead, seek to *respond* from your desired state of being (e.g. calm, guiding or open-minded). In time, your old reactions (e.g. aggression or defensiveness) will be replaced, quite naturally, by those that demonstrate your new state of being.

5. True spiritual growth inevitably creates change in you and your life. If you're not interested in change (for example if you're happy with things as they are) then understand that you limit your spiritual development.

CHAPTER 9

—————▼—————

Why is mankind's progress to enlightenment so slow, and why have the previous masters had so little global impact?

How are you measuring progress with this? Time? Speed? Would you feel better if everyone in the world was progressing *faster* toward enlightenment?

Well, yes. Isn't that the right idea?

Your underlying objective here, for all people to be enlightened, is a fair one. But the purpose of your world is for God to experience himself through the embodiment of what he is not.

Whoa! So God does not want peace and everyone enlightened?

That's not what I said. His desire is peace[7], and he knows that to be inevitable. In fact, it has already happened since all events have already played out. However, in your "meantime" of today, the world plays out so that all possibilities in your three dimensions can be explored, and within this, time is required, and therefore will seem to be passing by for all participants in the duration of all potentialities. You need to not think about time, but instead what we told you about "experience volume". There has been a great

---

7 The intended meaning of "peace" here is foundational in the subsequent development - and conclusions - of these dialogues.

volume created and there is more yet for you to experience, as you choose.

It seems odd that God would have us experience the bad stuff at all, but I understand why. But can't he hurry it along?

Again, time is not real. All possible experiences must occur (and already have) but to make them real in your world, time has to appear to pass and the Players must be fully immersed in the events. God therefore cannot speed the events along since time does not exist - except in making the events seem real in three-dimensional experiences.

That makes me think of something - Is this related to why we cannot seem to work out how we can "go back in time"? Many people would like to be able to do so - to avoid some of the tragic events of the past, for example.

Since all events have already been played out, end to end, all you could do is to visit one of the other potentialities where your bad event never happened or was avoided – or alternatively, experience a good event that did not occur in your current potentiality. Once in the other potentiality, you would simply play along with the event as it happens there, and change nothing in your original potentiality. In addition, God does not need to experience something more than once. He (and therefore you) has no purpose in creating a way to re-experience any event - all possibilities have happened and experiences gained. And what God does not create, you cannot create.

Fascinating, but off my original point... back to my question. If the previous masters were right, then why is mankind where it is?

Mankind is not your issue. This is a matter of where YOU are, in relation to the mankind and the world you create in order to create a higher self. You are here to create, not follow a process and/or learn what someone else can teach you.   The master you know best is Jesus, so I could use him to explain this to you.

Yes, he's a good example - but sorry to be negative... look what he seems to have created, indirectly: Crusades, bigotry and an excuse for horrors such as the Inquisition. Now the war in Iraq is becoming a religious war.

That unfortunate perspective comes from the human condition of first receiving the messenger, then his/her followers, then the media of the message, and finally losing sight of the message itself. For example, Jesus' teachings were swiftly turned into a message about Jesus, "The Messiah". Then it became a message about the book of his teachings (the Bible), and finally a message that this book and Jesus Himself were the only way to God. Along the way, Jesus' actual teachings took second place to the power attributed to the guru, the rulebook, and the religious powerhouses that sprung from them.

So what do we do about it?

Listen - it's not about "we" or "do". Let me say it again: It's NOT about "we" or "do". This is critically important. It's about what YOU will BE having heard:
a) The messages from the masters - allowing for misinterpretation over time.
b) These lessons from us - allowing for your own human limitations and filters in hearing and writing down and understanding what we are telling you here.
As we have said, you cannot change other people, and there's nothing you can do in this world to make it perfect. But you can, by becoming an ever higher version of yourself, perfect your own part of the world by perceiving it differently, and in doing so, help others change themselves and their perspective.

So, it's all down to <u>me</u> then?

Who else could it be down to?

A new Spiritual Master, perhaps? Someone I can learn more from and follow?

You know all there is, and are remembering more of it each day. There are new masters and have been many, but you must lead yourself. Masters are guides, and differ from the *Observers* we discussed earlier in these exchanges in that they take the impartial observation, depthless love, and unending forgiveness into participation in the game again, but live there with that enlightenment, and the power (and risk) that brings.

Hold on - So there are now *four* stages then: Player, Spectator, Observer, and Master. Like a continuum, right? So we, sorry, I, make my way along this line, from left to right?

In a way, yes. But you can be (and are) in different places - simultaneously. Let go of time and remember your earthly lives are about volume of *experience* as we have described. Remember that your life is the creation of events that you can experience from any one of these four stages, once you know about them. Most people in your current life are fully immersed Players, and many do not even know, in the human life in which you observe them that there are other stages. This is deliberate because in that way they can play out their potentiality, and enable the plan of God to be.

Plan of God - is there one big plan then, all written up, as it were?

If you mean is it limited in its possibilities, then no. God's plan is everything that could be. It is beautiful in its complexity and possibilities. Since it has everything, it cannot be anything but perfect and complete.

OK. Go on.

Now, within this particular potentiality, your life as you are experiencing it, you chose to gain awareness, and as a consequence are now learning and showing readiness to move more and more of your conscious *experience* to the right of your continuum. But do not forget:

a) All your previous (and future) lives (and the potentialities of this one) are happening in parallel, as are those of others.

b) Everyone really knows *everything*... So in the other parallel lives, you and others may have chosen to be in different stages than the ones in which you operate in this life. In some lives and potentialities you are a fully immersed Player.

So, think on this, Simon – Whatever others may do, do not look down on or judge them. Instead, see that their being a Player in total immersion (and honesty) is a gift to you, so that <u>you</u> can choose to be a higher self in relation to them and fulfill your role in this life/potentiality. Tie to this the knowledge that everyone is the ultimately the same being, and part of God, then how could you do anything but love your fellow man, every one?

Hold on – I just can't bring myself to love the murderer, the tyrant, the robber...

That is true for you only if you see them from the perspective of the Player, wherein you are part of the game - and will judge them. But when you know that they are Players, playing out roles by which you can learn what <u>you</u> are from what they are not, you can love them just as you love a Hollywood actor, even if she always plays the parts of the villain. As Shakespeare wrote *"All the world's a stage, and all the men and women merely players"*. Until you can see your world this way, you will indeed be unable to love and accept everyone, or even *anyone*. Your expectations of people will be too high and sooner or later they will seem to let you down, fall off their pedestal.

Well. I do have a tendency to have expectations of others that they cannot maintain. That is true of relationships in love, work and also religions, actually.

And has that worked for you?

No. I end up being disappointed. And actually, I now tend just to assume right up front that everyone will let me down – cannot be trusted.

Maybe you can change that now.

Indeed - I'm beginning to think that I should be more appreciative of the "bad" people in my life; because it's from them I can measure my own progress to a higher self!

That is a big step, Simon; a great moment of insight.

Ah. I think I am getting it. But let me step back a bit, thinking about me in comparison to others and the four stages. Is my volume of experience greater than that of others, then?

It's not a matter of experience quantity in the three-dimensional way you would usually think of it. It's a matter of the development of the role in becoming a porthole for God to see through in each life (potentiality) in which you participate. In this life, you are playing more stages than you do in others, and observing more for God. As we said earlier in these materials, you've experienced enough in *this* life to be ready for what God needs you back for. And this is it. This will provide a new opportunity for you as you complete this life.

Yes, but what is it he needs me for, exactly? When will I get to do it?

You're doing it already by learning to BE something else. Don't seek a great mission, or act, or monumental service. Indeed, many such acts are usually driven by Players with great egos, and are nothing to do with the individual's higher self or God. Your task is not to DO anything, but to experience and learn what you came into this life for. Simply hear us and seek to be a higher version of yourself and whatever that entails doing, will follow. God is not about big egotistical human tasks and achievements - quite the opposite. Despite the popular saying, *God, not the devil, is in the detail.*

OK... But give me a place to start.

You have already started. You are here, now. Simon, don't miss out on recognizing your progress. You are doing what God wanted you back for, and he wanted your attention, not your time. It's a matter of continuing along. You are at a transitional stage, and many events will require you to change your psychological points of departure as you respond to and plan your life experience. Below are some key differences to help you understand and respond to situations as they come up:

Instead of...	Strive For...
Doing	Being
Being a Player	Spectating and Observing
Judging	Understanding and Forgiving
Learning	Remembering and application
Age and time	Experience
Faith in Doctrine	Trust in Self
Confidence in Knowing	Comfort in Not Knowing
Things	Nothing (no-thing)

There are many others, and these are simplifications, but they are given to help.

OK, but wait a minute. This exchange is a big moment - it's hard to trust what I have concluded: The task for which God "wants me back" is really just this very period of spiritual (or whatever it is) development - in itself?

What finer mission could you have?

Yes, I see. I need to be OK with this self-centered thing, right?

Yes. And forget not that as you become your higher self, you will become very busy, because "As soon as you decide who and what you are everything unlike it will come into the space" (Walsch, Bringers of the Light, 1995 p. 53) and by your new being, so will your new doing manifest.

I understand. Again, I have to learn to 'let go' I guess. I have to learn to be.

Review

1. There are four levels of human consciousness in the world:
    a. Player (fully immersed)
    b. Spectator (watching but heavily vested in the outcomes)
    c. Observer (watching as an independent witness)
    d. Master (enlightened observers, able to participate with Players but maintaining detachment).

2. If you observe someone you consider a 'Player' behaving in a way of which you disapprove, don't condemn him. His total immersion (and honesty) in his role is a gift enabling you to be your higher self... *in relation to them*.

3. Your life mission need not be to complete a great mission or famous deed - which is often only a need of the ego and nothing to do with your life purpose. Your task is to experience and find out what you came here to learn – which may be something small in the big scheme of things!

CHAPTER 10

▼

What next?

Are you being what you desire to be?

Yes. Well, as best I can. Am I failing?

You cannot fail. The important thing is that you are now aware, most of the time, of what you want to be and what you are thinking and doing: *You are observing yourself.* Sometimes you are then modifying yourself to be what you want to be in relationship to what is occurring. Other times you are just aware of yourself doing what comes naturally, and watch yourself to see how you are progressing. Other times you are lost in playing Simon Watson.

I guess I am being a Spectator and a Player too much, then.

As an Observer you can watch the activities not only of others but of you yourself, amid the game. But you still have to participate. It's not about withdrawal, but rather about not being sucked in and getting lost as a Player. Indeed, to withdraw to complete Observation would mean removal of yourself from normal participation in life, which you can do, but you might not find practical - or even very much fun.

Hold on – you spent a lot of time telling me about this... about <u>not</u> participating in the game. This is contradictory!

No, not contradictory, just the next layer of understanding. As an Observer you can observe yourself as both the Player and even Spectator. The point is that you are not lost in the apparent reality – you are fully conscious as the Observer.

I'm getting confused here: Should I participate or not?

You can, as and when it serves you to do so. Now that we have had these discussions, you are able to participate <u>on your own terms</u>, with the background awareness of the true nature of your world. You now have the knowledge that will enable you to choose whether to become fully lost in the illusion again, knowing what it is, its purpose, and how you can then use the experiences to your own ends.

But if I was to use the world to my own ends, does that not require total immersion?

Total immersion gives control of consciousness to your ego and/or the collective conscious to create the environment in which you find yourself and your experience therein. If you avoid total immersion, modification of your behavior and responses enables you to use the environment as a crucible in which you can experiment with what you want to be in relationship to the physical experience and surroundings you create.

This is very hard to get my head around...

Yes. This is why we provide this information to you in pieces.

Let me try to summarize what you're telling me: It's not about me trying to be different in the world as it happens around me, to show what I truly am. Instead, it's about me being constantly aware of the true nature of the world and then creating and interacting

with it in a way that I use my physical experience to *test out what I believe I am or desire to be* **in relation to that world.**

Yes.

I don't feel I have that much control.

Indeed. And that's the issue at hand, here.

I see. OK - How does the "being and doing" thing fit in here, then? I thought it was about being, and then the doing happens.

That was a simplification. You create your environment and experiences based on your vision of your desired BEING - the doing then happens around you, and you respond to it - to demonstrate what you are and measure your growth to a higher version of yourself. Indeed, the environment you create may not be the same as your desired state of being; it may be quite the opposite. It's that way by design, so that you can prove and test and experience what it is that you are in relativity to what you are not.

Wait! So you're saying that if I want to be calm and guiding, for example, then the experience I create around me might be just the opposite?

Yes. Although you will also find that if you can recognize, observe and accept the experience, your struggle, and the conditions will resolve.

But I thought that the whole point was to create my own reality – so I would be in a place where I can be what I want to be, i.e. a place where two of my desired states, calmness and guiding, prevail.

What purpose would that serve?

I would be happy and content!

Were these two of your desired states of being?

Uh, no.

It does not matter. Where would your growth come from if your environment were a place where everything around you was already what you want to be? Do you not see that to be those things, you need at least some of the time, to be in an environment NOT like that - where you can practice, hone and develop your desired state of being?

This is not good... You mean that I create an environment in which I will have to struggle - deliberately? What is the point of that?

It's the very point of the world. But as we just said, you will find that if you can recognize observe and accept the experience, your struggle, and the conditions will resolve. Also know that when you leave this world, you can create all the happiness and contentment you could possibly imagine, if that's what you desire.

Oh No! So the world <u>is</u> about struggle, and misery and strife!

Let's say it's about work and challenge. *But not because some cruel God or Creator wanted to torture poor Souls!* Listen again: The purpose of human existence is for you to create physical experiences against which to test your desired state of being.

As Eckhart Tolle wrote: "Is suffering really necessary? Yes and no. If you had not suffered as you have, there would be no depth to you, no humility, no compassion."

Indeed. You do this as part of, and for God to experience Himself. To do so, you (and others) create and participate in an experience that can be the opposite of your desired state of being, so that you can physically experience what you want to be - in relation to what you are not. As you develop this knowledge and ability, you can use your unlimited creative abilities to temper the amount of opposition you create to yourself; along with using the strength that knowing this is not "real" provides to handle the challenges. You can literally create a "better life" once you cease to be at the will of the creative powers of the collective conscious. That said, you will always be impacted by the collective unconscious to some extent, especially if the prevailing tone is opposite to your own.

But, are you saying that people who have really <u>horrible</u> lives actually wanted it that way?

It's what we have said all along. Now I am saying that they chose to experience that kind of life because that was the level of challenge they set for themselves. Many of them remain unaware (in their human consciousness) of what you are learning here, and believe that they are swept along on the tides of fate. Yet in reality they are learning exactly what it was they set out to learn. You, and others like you, on the other hand, are aware of your ability to influence your experience, and now you know a little more about why.

This seems to address my worries about the apparent greediness of those who push the laws of attraction and creative visualization etc. I feel better about those powers now.

Your creative powers are not for you to be greedy and lazy (unless that's what you want to experience) but for you *to create the environment in which to have the experiences you seek*. This is part of the true meaning of Free Will. There are those who have learned some of the powers to create abundance (mainly wealth) but do not, in this life, know or effectively share the *reason* for the existence of this creative power. So they appear to be seeking and preaching about getting something for nothing. Of course, this is what they have chosen to experience, so no-one is really at fault.

Why am I learning this now if others are not?

Because you choose to know this, now, as do those who read this.

What about other lives? Did I want and have the same knowledge in past lives? And will I remember it in future lives?

Remember, all your lives have happened already in a vertical not linear manner, each one a potentiality. Your current level of awareness was your choice in this particular potentiality. And all of your experiences add up to your total entity.

If it's all already played out, doesn't it make this all a bit pointless? Why can't I just fast-forward to the end?

Because this dialogue was and is part of your potentiality; part of your experience and your contribution to God. There is still more to play out, and you have to see it through. You will just do so with more awareness than most others in this potentiality.

Review

1. Spiritual awareness presents an opportunity to know the true nature of the world, and to use your physical experiences to test out what you believe you are or desire to be in relation to that world.

2. The environment and experience you create around yourself will at times be the opposite of your desired state of being. This enables you to practice, hone and develop yourself. Once you recognize, observe and accept the experience, your struggle, and the conditions can resolve. Remind yourself often of the Hebrew phrase "Gam zeh ya'avor - This too shall pass."

3. This experience, and the rest of your life (*whatever* you do), is part of your contribution to God. In gaining awareness through these lessons you can contribute with more awareness than many others around you.

CHAPTER 11

▼

So, I can create anything, based on my own level of faith. That sounds familiar. But here's my problem: I cannot try to be a higher being and use that gift because by trying to be so, I am defining my lack of that level, just the same as wanting creates only more wanting. I just am where I am. What do I do then?

You said it. You are where you are.

That's no help! How do I get to the next point?

By being there.

Come on - This is a silly circle. I am where I am, so I cannot be more. And I cannot be more until I already am. Sorry but that's just a riddle.

Yes it is, if you approach it from a perspective of doing separated from being.

Are we just back to "being" and "doing" then? I have already said what I want to be! Oops... What I <u>desire</u> to be. I really do see the importance of not "wanting".

Are you ready for the next step then?

Sure. That's what this is all about.

Until you believe *you already are* the list of things you stated you desire to be, then the list remains just that: A list. You cannot develop spiritually by doing anything in a contrived way, but you can develop by living with the genuine and instinctual responses to your daily life that stem from your desired state of being. Observance of such behavior is the origin of the religious view of being "watched" by God. The difference is that God is not judging you, but being there, through you, as the impartial Observer.

You mean I have to be naturally and instinctively in line with my desired state of being in <u>all</u> my responses and actions? That's impossible – too much to ask, isn't it? How could I ever achieve that?

Stop thinking that the change is instant. Be prepared to work at it. That's what this world is about.

Explain, please.

Let's use Golf as an analogy. It's a good example because as a sport, Golf is played alone and it has specific pinnacles of achievement that every person could attain just by themselves – zero handicaps, Professional status, Open Champion, etc.

OK. I see that. Go on.

Do most new players achieve a natural golf swing by first learning what an apparently unnatural position, grip and motion they must adopt? And do they learn these as a new routine, checking off these items as they address each and every swing?

Yes.

And do those who go on to improve eventually do these things without thinking about them – they become automatic?

Yes, I suppose so.

So why would it be different with spiritual growth?

Spirituality is more, well, mental or abstract, isn't it?

What makes someone become a great golfer?

Well, they get training from a Professional. And they persevere through the failures and discomfort until the motions of the game become second nature to them. And they practice a lot!

OK. What would happen if they just sat and read a book about golf? Or only tried it once or twice?

They would be able to *talk* about golf, but not *play* it... Mmmm.

Indeed... And what makes some golfers keep on going and learning and love the sport... and then even make a living from it?

They play it enough?

More than that! They begin to experience what it feels like to be good at it. They begin to see and feel the benefits, experience their progress. And this can only be done by desiring to excel and by practicing over and over and over again until at last they believe they are a good player, and then, then, they really are! One day they stand on the course and know they are a great player. And they got there by *being a golfer* over and over and over again, and always with an insatiable desire to be better, to reach that lower handicap.

But some people never play it well... They just aren't cut out for it.

Then they become something else. Something they are cut out for, or desire more. Just like <u>your</u> experience with golf.

I understand, and that helps a lot. But you said I can't progress through DOING anything, but this seems to contradict that.

The act of doing - without that doing being based on manifestation of a deeply desired state of being or without a faith and discipline that creates a natural progression and change - achieves nothing. But by desiring to be better, by practicing (with the successes and failures that brings) you create the experiences that will enable you one day to KNOW that you have become what you wanted to be. Or decide to be something else.

This all sounds very practical and, well, somewhat unspiritual if I may say so!

"Practical" is what the worldly experience is about. And practical action does not demonstrate a lack of spiritual knowledge[8]. You will achieve no growth in the physical elements of the human world by thinking alone. On the other hand, spiritual growth enables you to manifest what you learn. You do this by using the creative powers you hold and by interacting with the physical world as it is and as you create it, in line with your desired state of being.

So I do have to <u>do</u> things... This is hard to grasp. Let me try to get this straight. I have to do things – but choose them by knowing what I want to be. By knowing what I want to be, I create an environment in which I can make that being a reality by doing things that manifest my desired state of being. My head is spinning.

---

8 I have since learned that we shouldn't discount the practical actions and solutions we need (e.g. jobs, insurance or medical help) as unspiritual and therefore inferior. We must operate in this world within our level of spiritual development (at any one time). And, when we take practical help available to us, we should avoid considering ourselves insufficiently spiritually evolved - because that just creates guilt - which is highly detrimental to our efforts for spiritual development (Jennings, Science of Mind Vol. 81 No. 5, 2008).

Go on.

And as you said in an earlier conversation, sometimes the created environment will be counter to my desired state of being, and that is by design: Because such relativity is required for me to see how I am doing and thus test and temper my growth.

Your understanding is growing. And now we have a question about your friend, RC. He had a full career as a Firefighter and Fire Chief, then became a college professor, and is now an attorney... a full life indeed. Now, if you were to ask him the following questions, what would he say?

- Did he reach the end of his career as a firefighter, knowing that he had been what he desired to be within those experiences?
- Did his next (and comparatively short-lived) career in college teaching enable him to be what he wanted to be - or more specifically, help him discover what he did NOT want to do?
- Is his new career as a lawyer providing him with the ability to do a job that enables him to be what he desires?

I think he would answer "Yes" to all three questions.

Compared to most, RC has made his life an abundance of opportunities to do things that enable him to try out what he desires to be.

That's great!

This is why people who love their jobs never tire of them until they die or get what they wanted from them. They see no gap between work and leisure time because they are doing what enables them to be what they want to be, and become better and better at it with every moment.

Review

1. Until you believe you already are what you desire to be, you will remain unchanged. You must develop that belief by living with the genuine and instinctual responses to your daily life that stem from your desired state of being (healthy, helpful, loving or perhaps, spiteful* - whatever you choose to be).

2. You know you have changed when you begin to experience what it <u>feels</u> like to be what you desire to be; when you begin to see and feel the benefits. That takes practice. In the meantime, what feelings did you have most TODAY? Those represent the being you are now.

3. People who love their jobs do so because they are doing things that come from or are congruent with what they desire to be.

* Note: Are you thinking "Well, of course it's easier to believe I can be spiteful"? That's because most people expect gratitude from those they help - whereas those being spiteful do not expect approval of any kind. The simple lesson is this: **If you remove your need for validation, approval or gratitude from others, it's easier to be what you want to be.**

CHAPTER 12

▼

I need some clarity about the Player/Spectator/Observer/Master stages. If I understand what you have said, the object is not to be a disconnected Observer, because that would end our ability to learn and develop by participating in the world (i.e. defeat the very purpose of the world). Is that correct?

You can choose.

So it's OK to just observe?

Yes - if that will enable you to become the next highest version of yourself.

But I can also be a Player?

Yes, if that's what you choose. But now you can be a Player with the ability to be *an Observer of yourself.* The point is that you are now conscious of the different roles.

Isn't that the same as being a Spectator, as you called it?

No. Spectators are still "unconscious" – they are vested in the end result of the game and will dispense judgment of the Players and events. However, being a Spectator is a necessary stepping stone to being an Observer, and is a first step in leaving total immersion in the illusion. When ready, a Spectator can move on to being an Observer.

Go on.

As an Observer, you become fully conscious and see the game for what it is. You end your conviction that the game is the only and final reality, and see the true purpose of the world. As *A Course in Miracles* puts it, you choose to see the world differently. Next, you can simultaneously be a Player and Observer, at which point you're not totally vested in the result of the game, but you play, do your part, and use the experiences to test out your grandest ideas about yourself. Yet you also know that it is not real and that your task is to observe yourself and the events and remain 'conscious'.

That sounds impossible – how can you avoid getting sucked back into events?

It is difficult... but to know that you can do it is the greatest part of the challenge - and this you have already achieved!

OK, so a Master can survive the "temptation", as it were. But surely a budding Observer cannot do so 100% of the time?

As we said, it is difficult. And hence in the Lord's Prayer you say "Lead us not into Temptation". Use it when you need to.

OK.

We see examples of this struggle in the story of Jesus where he threw the traders from the temple; and in his final moments when cried out, "My God, My God, why hast thou forsaken me?" But the true master moves past these moments and returns to their perspective of Master and Observer, as did Jesus when he said, "Father, forgive them, for they know not what they do".

Yes, I understand that. I have a long way to go... But that makes me a bit despondent.

Remember that you cannot fail because you have already succeeded. All possibilities have already happened. Your awareness of your human journey and efforts are necessary only in that you must experience them within the construct of human time for them to be valid.

Please explain...

Is your despondence because you feel it will take this and other lifetimes to achieve mastery? That you don't want to struggle with this for an infinite time?

Yes, exactly that.

As we have said, if you can change your concept of time, things will be much clearer. Let us try to put it this way: Firstly, your Soul's many lifetimes have already run through every potentiality, simultaneously. This fact you now know. Secondly, you, in the partition of your Soul you know as Simon Watson, are aware only of your human life as Simon. You know only one life at a time. You do not face having to go through hundreds or thousands of lives one after the other to achieve mastery and return to God. All you have to do is see this experience, the life and times of Simon Watson, through to conclusion at which time all the other potentialities will also be concluded. When they are over, which they already are, you will return to your greater self, your Soul, just as your Soul will, when it is ready, return to its greater self.

I get it! But what happens when I return to my greater self?

Your greater self chooses what it wants to do, create more experiences or, as we said, return to oneness with God.

But that sounds like time to me: Time between lives, as it were, when the Soul is working out what to do next.

Try to think of it as events, rather than a period of time, and that it's happening NOW rather than in the past or future. Right now your Soul is creating the lives it wants to experience, and Simon Watson is one of them. If you could look at the Soul from the macro level, where time does not exist, you would see all of its human lives have played out, and the Soul could be seen as in a steady state. But if you were to look down into the micro level of the Soul, there is huge activity as lives play out in what seems, within them, to be periods of time.

You mean time only occurs at the micro level of the Soul? Down here, in each of our human lives? You mean if one could step back, you'd no longer see all the detailed activities, but just see the whole, the Soul?

Yes. And if you looked around, you would see all the other Souls, all interacting and busy with their own evolution.

Wait, does that mean that the Souls are actually another micro level and if I took yet another step back, I would see another macro level of apparent steady state? It's like a series of concentric circles.

On and on into eternity... And every Soul does this until such a time that it has experienced all that it needs and returns to oneness with God. It chooses to end its individuality.

Wow. That sounds like looking into an atom or the like. Or like looking up at space and being awed at the thought that it goes on for eternity.

Indeed.

I'm getting dizzy thinking about it. Hold on again. I cannot help

thinking that there is some degree of time involved in the evolution of the Soul, yet you keep asking me to believe time is not real.

Our point is that time as you know it (and particularly all the limitations it creates) is not relevant beyond your human experience. For you, it is a critical component in making your human experience valid and comprehendible. The problem with human time is that unless you can let it go as an eternal truth, it makes understanding the bigger picture impossible to grasp. Our intent is to enable you to let go of time as you understand it and be able to see that eternity is not constrained by it.

Review

1. The line in the Lord's Prayer "Lead us not into Temptation" can help us with the struggle we all face with remaining an Observer when being pulled back into the game to become an unconscious Player. Say it out loud when you feel it happening and it will give you strength.

2. Your Soul's many lifetimes have already run through every potentiality, simultaneously, and are concluded from God's perspective. You (the person reading this) know only your one life (although some people have glimpses of others) on behalf of your Soul. You do not face having to go through hundreds or thousands of lives, one after the other, to achieve mastery and return to God. All you have to do is see this life through.

3. Your Soul has many lives/experiences (of which you are one) at the macro level. Activity and time occur at the micro level of a Soul (for example in your human life and consciousness), but at the macro level, there is a steady state. Think of it as observing atoms within an apparently solid object.

CHAPTER 13

▼

If you're so intertwined with me, why do I make mistakes? And for that matter, how is that free will?

There are two questions there. Firstly, we'll answer regarding free will: This is the easier answer for you to understand. You ask us for guidance because you desire to do so, and desire to do so because we are all in this together. Having listened to us, <u>you</u> then choose what to do in the physical experience, even after you have considered our perspective. It's wholly your own decision. Thus you retain "Free Will".

But why would I ignore your input? You're God, kind of, right?

You don't ignore us as such, you simply choose to hear us and then make a decision based on what <u>you</u> want to experience. In this way you are like a child, and so it should be. For example, have you consistently done EVERYTHING that we have advised in all these *written* exchanges?

Well, no.

OK. So, about still making mistakes after hearing our perspective: Do you assume that if you ask us for guidance that we will (or even desire to) give you an answer that would enable you to avoid every mistake? Always make the perfect decision, take the best action and always win?

Well, yes. Why else ask you?

Think again. We told you already there is no right or wrong – there just is. And do you remember that you already know everything and that learning is only remembering what you already know?

Yes.

Again, we know what you know because we are not separate from you - we are one. However, our apparent separateness from you is helpful in your human consciousness because it assists you in making the most out of your physical life experiences, and in these dialogues especially, this apparent separation helps you get clarification on what you are beginning to remember. Yet there is no true separation, and thus we are part of your thoughts and reasoning as you move about in the usual day to day activities.

Now, as for "mistakes", there are no such things. There is only the result you have chosen in order to experience what you desired, and that may be something labeled a success or a failure, depending on your viewpoint. It's also worth considering that <u>your</u> failure is often another man's success. Also consider that there is no finite time, and <u>you</u> decide on each potentiality you experience, and can, if you wish, live every one of them through to each and every success and failure ending. These are just potentialities, and at any one human moment, you are aware of only one of them; one potential outcome: The one you wanted to experience, now.

Wow. There is no such thing as a failure... there's only ever the *possibility* of one, as an experiential event. And even then it's relative...

You just *"Live the is that you have chosen"*.

I like that: *"Live the is that you have chosen"*. Can I use it?

Sure. You wrote it.

I guess I did. Anyhow, let me clarify - your role is to help me decide which potentiality to choose, then?

No. We are part of what you are and know, and are part of the way you learn and experience yourself. We're more of a sounding board, as you might call it. For many people we are just an undifferentiated part of their thought process. But for people like you, we become a more distinct entity, *a partner in the transition to being an Observer.*

So 'Players' do not know you (i.e. this part of themselves) at all?

No. In a way, you could say it's a way to *define* a Player – someone who cannot hear this aspect of themselves.

What about 'Spectators'?

They hear us, but seldom. But they do know of this aspect of themselves, whereas Players do not.

Review

1. Whoever you ask for guidance (your inner guides, your God, or whoever) don't assume you'll get an answer that will enable you to avoid every mistake or problem – you will experience what you came here for, good or bad, win or lose. Instead, seek support and help in dealing with and *learning* from the experience, in the moment.

2. If you are able to hear your inner guides or God (in whatever way that works for you!) you don't have to follow their direction – that's one element of "free will". But listen - and make the decision a <u>conscious</u> one.

3. There is no such thing as a mistake: There is only the result of your (often subconsciously) desired experience... and that may be something labeled a success or a failure, depending on your viewpoint. And remember that one person's failure is another person's success.

CHAPTER 14

▼

If we choose our own journeys and outcomes, then why do we experience sadness and accidents and sorrow and death? As my friend RC said to me, he sure never chooses those. So, the fact that he experiences them means he does not have free will. True?

When you say "he sure never chooses those", who is the "he" to whom you refer?

Himself - RC Bunger. When he experiences something bad, he can definitely tell himself "I did not choose this".

So he means his human consciousness, his mind, did not choose the event?

Yes, I believe that's what he means.

The human mind is the awareness with which you experience the world as a real and irresistible series of events. As we have said before, you must believe that the events are real because otherwise they cease to have any value as an experience.

I'm not talking about needing to believe it's real, I understand that. I think the question is more why we have to experience anything bad at all – RC's point was that if we had free will then

we would not choose to experience <u>anything</u> unpleasant. Since we do experience such things, then we surely don't have free will.

There are two levels to free will. There is free will of Simon Watson the man, who exists only within all the constraints of the physical world. Simon is free to behave within and respond to his environment in any way he chooses. Then there is the free will of your Soul, the greater entity of which Simon Watson is a temporary and fleeting part. It is at the Soul level that the broader courses of action and events are chosen, and Simon Watson has nothing to do with that. Simon's job is to live out the events that his Soul has chosen, good and bad.

So I, Simon Watson, the only consciousness of which I am aware, have no free will then?

You're not listening. Yes you do have free will — to respond in whatever way you see fit to the experiences that unfold. Also, you have free will to do, physically, whatever you are capable of doing in the material world, within the desired experience of your Soul.

But what about events like someone close to me getting sick?

No, you do not choose that. But the other person does, and you are complicit with it at the Soul level of which you, Simon, have no direct knowledge. But you can choose how you respond to it in the material world.

I just can't believe people really <u>choose</u> to get sick.

At their Soul level and complicit with the other Souls, all of which are joined together to some extent, a Soul may choose for one of its physical manifestations to get sick as part of the desired experience. On the human consciousness level, they did not choose it, but again, the human has free will in how he or she responds to it.

This is hard to hear. It really seems that we are living our lives at

the whim of a greater being – not even God, but our own Soul! Is that fair?

It does not seem fair if you continue to want to cling to your individuality and specialness; if your ego cries out that it needs to survive and has been forsaken by everyone, everything, including God. This is the very challenge that *A Course in Miracles* points out: That until you see that nothing is real your task is only to relinquish your specialness. And all the while your ego will do all it can to stop you. Until you fully accept that, you will not understand.

Let me get this straight then. I, Simon, have free will to do what I want in the physical world, and to respond to its events in any way I choose. But I cannot choose what happens to me and those around me in order to avoid sadness and loss.

Now, again consider *A Course in Miracles*. It tells you that you cannot change the world, for that is not its purpose. Your task is to choose to see it differently and in giving up your specialness, in realizing that nothing here is real[9], you cease to need to have a perfect and safe life. You will never look about you and see only peace and beauty. But you can choose to see the world differently by seeing through the bad, knowing that all is illusion, and that you are not alone.

Yes, that is what it says. And I remember that this is an extraordinarily hard task, and that to succeed fully requires huge faith and the ability to defeat the ego and listen instead to the Holy Spirit.

Yes. And when you heard that it put you off the *Course*, didn't it?

Yes it did. I remember exactly where I was sitting when I heard it! But I feel better about it now because I have more faith about

---

9 "Nothing here is real" means this life experience is not a finite reality where death means either extinction or a place in heaven if you have been good enough.

the alternative and less reliance on the ego. It seems possible to me now that what happens here in this world does not matter in the way I thought it did, and that I don't have to listen to the ego and its desperate attempts to keep me separate. I even feel some sympathy for the ego.

Yes. The ego is very busy protecting what it thinks is the real and only you.

Wait a minute. Then I don't really have free will at all if I am listening to my ego.

You <u>are</u> your ego until such a time as you break away from it. Once you begin to seek enlightenment then you distance yourself from the ego and recognize it for what it is. That is the purpose of *A Course in Miracles*. You become closer to your Soul and gain access to God. Now, you, Simon, are most of the time not blindly doing your ego's bidding. But many people are.

So I guess that's why what some people do with their "free will" is what I consider bad or unpleasant... interesting. Summarize for me, then.

Your Soul has free will to define what it wants to experience through physical matter, bodies and minds - humans. Then at a second level, your mind and body have free will to behave and respond to those environments and experiences. Now, there is likely to be a close relationship between what the Soul intended the mind and body to do and what it actually does, but not always – it depends on the level of connection between the Soul and the mind and body. Some are more aligned than others, and these varying states manifest in many different ways such as illnesses.

OK, so back to RC's point. He does NOT have free will in the way he wants it, right?

If he means he wants to be able always to choose the happy path and avoid problems then no, he has no control over that *from purely the physical or body level*. But for those who are attuned more harmoniously with the Soul, the mind can bridge the gap, and hence tap into the creative powers of the Soul and affect the physical world to some extent. The true masters not only achieve this attunement but also bridge across from the Soul to the greater oneness that is God.

I think RC considers that if he cannot control the events of his life, he does not have free will.

We have explained this already. And if he wishes and is ready to, he can work on bridging the gap between his mind and his greater Soul, and thusly have more of the control he seeks. Perhaps he is still too vested in his separateness... many people you see about you are. And so it is and should be.

So let me summarize now. As Simon Watson, I have to accept that what I am experiencing I have chosen at a level of consciousness higher than my "mind and body". My "free will" as a human in the physical reality is simply what I do and how I react day to day within the framework of my Soul's creation. However, if I can bridge the gap back between my mind and my Soul, I can tap the creative power of God and have much greater influence over my world. I can do this by the various techniques out there such as laws of attraction etc. but I first have to be willing and able to release myself from my immersion and belief in my individual specialness and separateness.

It's very important that you see that bridging back to your Soul is not about making radical changes to the Soul's intent and plan. If you achieve the connection, you will understand your Soul's purpose and therefore your own - and you will shift from resistance to acceptance.

I understand, but it is still hard to grasp that my life is largely pre-

defined, especially given I feel quite in control of it... In fact, I feel even more in control as a result of these dialogues.

Consider this. Imagine your child is about to fall into a fire. In order to save him, you make a decision (very quickly) on what to do and as it turns out, you are going to have to burn your hand. You would do so, right?

Yes, of course.

Would you expect your hand to refuse to do it?

No, I expect, as part of me, my hand would do what was needed based on the overall decision that I was making with my brain.

Indeed. Now, can you see a parallel with you and your Soul? If your hand was burned in the scenario we describe, would it subsequently feel annoyed at being harmed by a predetermined decision by your brain?

No. It plays its part, and I then do my best to heal it. But hold on - my hand does not have a life and consciousness of its own, does it?

Everything has a level of consciousness of some kind, and independent reactions go beyond physical attachment to the originating host. For example, as you learned in Deepak Chopra's *The Spontaneous Fulfillment of Desire*, he states that scientists have proven that human cells continue to react to stimuli from the host human body even after separation from it.

So you're saying that I should just go along with my Souls' plan?

We're saying that, on the whole, you do – but you can choose how to respond to events, and that response will be different given your new insights here. Listen: You need to accept that you are creating what's happening to you, but at a different level than your human consciousness. Now, if you can bridge back to your Soul, you'll understand that fully - and by being connected to that greater consciousness, you'll realize that you truly already are creating what you desire. And you, Simon, the human, are experiencing that creation; touching and sensing the world for God - like a cell on his fingertip.

I think I am beginning to understand.

Review

1. There are two levels of 'free will':

    a. The free will of your Soul, the greater entity of which you are a temporary and fleeting part. It is at the Soul level that broader potentialities are chosen

    b. Your (human) free will to respond to the experiences that unfold and to do, physically, whatever you are capable of doing in the material world

2. Your level of enlightenment is reflected in the level of awareness and acceptance you have of this fact, and how you respond to your experiences.

    There is usually a close relationship between what the Soul intended the mind and body to do and what the latter actually does, but not always – it depends on the level of connection between the three. Some are more aligned than others, and these varying states manifest in many different ways such as illnesses and other effects of dis-ease.

3. You are creating what's happening to you, but at a different level than your human consciousness – at your Soul level. If you can reconnect to your Soul, you'll understand that fully - and by being connected to that greater consciousness, you'll realize that you truly already are creating what you desire. You, in your human experience are physically experiencing human life on behalf of your Soul – and God. And that's what the world is for.

CHAPTER 15

▼

You said that free will is on two levels, the first being that of the Soul who creates the basis from which the human body and mind then execute their free will. So, just how far ahead does the Soul plan: A day, a year, a whole life?

As we have discussed, there is only now. All potentialities have already played out, good and bad, happy and sad. All of them, in a "grand plan" as it were. So, given that, the whole plan has been made, and indeed has been completed. What you are experiencing is just one of those potentialities and it's totally real to you and has to be that way for the plan to have played out with any meaning.

When I hear that I feel that this life is just a waste of time... that this is just a silly masquerade and we're all puppets.

If you are a 'Player', then that might be a way to look at it, but you're not. And a fully immersed Player would not believe this anyway. Again, your life has to have seemed like a real experience for you to have played your part in making the "grand plan" fulfill its purpose of exploring the potentialities of what is not God. That feels like a waste of time to you because you realize that you never really had the independence and singular significance that you thought you had. Remember your role in the grand plan. As you know, Gandhi said "Whatever you do will be insignificant, but it is very important that you do it."

I am just part of a predetermined game then?

No. 'Predetermined' suggests that a specific outcome was defined and then acted out with other possibilities avoided or denied. That's not the case here in that EVERY possible outcome is a potentiality. No possibility is missed. Each Soul and each human used its free will to decide on courses of action until, eventually there were no more to play through.

Hold on! Just wait there! How can there be a limit on this? How can there be no more possibilities? If there were, there would be a limit on God!

That's a great point. The explanation we give you regarding playing out of all possibilities is in terms that you understand and are comfortable with. But since you ask, indeed, there is no limit, and the potentialities do go on forever.

Oh no, I'm lost then. So has everything played out or not?

Yes, but not in terms of a finite number of events or time. It just is played out. It has no end, there is only now. The only limitation to the omniverse is the awareness of the Souls or entities within it, and these are constantly changing and growing so that it all expands continuously. *The only way to consider any kind of ending is to consider that the ending is the limit of the Souls in what they can understand and create.*

That doesn't work for me - They are God – He has no limits and understands everything.

Here's a dichotomy: They are God, but they are not. They are parts of God with which God can experience Himself, and to do that they have to not be part of God. So, they do have a boundary but that boundary expands constantly.

Oh boy. So then, how does this answer my initial question?

A Soul does not plan an ending, because it has no concept of an ending since it constantly expands. Again, a Soul uses the human existence as part of its role of God experiencing Himself. It does it in many ways, one being human existences, all simultaneously, as it extends itself and learns.

You see, the Soul does not have a plan for you in the way you might want it to (like a parent or a boss) since you are only a small part of it, and play a role within it – just as a cell does in your body. While you continue to believe in your own separateness and specialness, you will demand that the Soul give you what you want, take care of you etc. When you can release that expectation, be the Observer, accept that the world is an exercise in self discovery by God, then you will be "enlightened", and if you want to, "ascend" beyond this human existence – bridging back to your Soul [more on this later]. And THAT is your truest moment of free will as a human. And that choice is always yours to take, although very few have done so fully.

So if I was to "ascend" then, would that be against the will of my Soul?

No, of course not! The decision to ascend would be the potentiality that you chose to follow, and that option is one that the Soul will have provided within the experiences that it laid out.

So who makes the choice – the Soul or me?

The Soul provides the possibility, but you choose it on the human level. And this is necessary for the potentiality to have occurred fully.

This is hurting my head. OK then, so why doesn't everyone just ascend?

Because most of them don't know what it even means – neither did you until now!

It really bothers me that all these people are running about so worried about what is really nothing. Such a waste of effort...and, well, rather embarrassing.

That's because you have empathy for their situation. And perhaps a sense of guilt that if you are right, if this dialogue is true, then you know what they should all know; that the world is not what it seems. But such a sense of guilt will only tie you to this world, and you need to let it go. Your purpose here is to define yourself, not others. And that purpose is being fulfilled, right now, just as are those of others. Your free will now is to choose differently, to choose to see the world differently, to move away from immersion in the game to reunite with your Soul and with all that truly is. You can do this when you are ready, perhaps after human death or before it.

Review

1. Your life must feel like a real and <u>singular</u> experience for you to have played your part in God's exploration of all potentialities. You now know that you are not a singular entity – and that flies in the face of your ego's demand that you are the most important thing in the world. See this as an opportunity to relieve yourself of the burden and fears your ego creates.

2. While you are only a small part of God's exploration, what you do, big or small, is an essential part of His plan:

   > "Whatever you do will be insignificant,
   > but it is very important that you do it."
   > – Gandhi.

3. The omniverse is the consciousness of the Souls or entities within it, and these are constantly changing and growing so that it all expands continuously.

4. Awareness of greater truth can bring with it a sense of guilt that everyone should know what you know. But such a sense of guilt only ties you into this world when you really need to let it go. Your purpose here is to define yourself, not others. And that purpose is being fulfilled, right here, right now.

CHAPTER 16

▼

I'm back to wondering who you are. Are you God, or his messengers of some kind?

If you are asking whether we are or from an entity that rules over everything and can give you supreme answers to all that is, then no. *God does not communicate His wishes because He does not have any.* He has no needs, demands, opinions, rules or anything else. God just is, and enables us all to be.

So who runs all this world stuff then?

That question comes from a traditional view of an all-powerful ruling God. After these dialogues, you don't really mean to ask if God runs the world do you? By now you know that everything is made up of multi-dimensional layers in which individual entities or Souls participate simultaneously. One of those dimensional layers is the world in which your Soul creates you, Simon Watson, to learn from physical experience. The central entity, or God as you call it, is that from which all the dimensions came, the originator and source. Be clear on that – *God enables us to be.* Your job is to choose what you want to be in relation to what you experience.

And your job?

We are like you, but we have a different role right now, that being to guide you, Simon.

Are you part of my bigger Soul, then?

Some of us are. Others are not. But remember that everything stems from the same source so no two Souls are truly separate. Everyone is 'related' via the Oneness.

How many are there of you?

We have no clear delineations such as those you are used to in the physical world. Also know that there are many dimensional layers and all have multiple potentialities in which Souls can participate. So we could be a trillion or just one, depending on how you look at it. Try not to think of us as people; we are not. You are not. Your waking consciousness, Simon Watson, is a single and temporary manifestation of your Soul as it learns and expands.

Is that it? We are just the fronds of a Soul, eh?

We, you, are the parts of God that have a perception of separateness from Him in order to be conscious and creative and learn in our own right and our own ways. So, you could say that in talking with us you _are_ talking at least to *parts* of God. As we have said, you enable God to experience Himself; you're one tiny part of all that is and ever was, and ever will be.

I sound somewhat insignificant when you put it like that.

There's that ego talking again. Let go of needing to be important in the grand scheme of things. Instead see yourself as a part of a huge and incredibly complex creation. The interesting thing is that even though you have a part in the grand plan, you are still completely free willed, yet your free will cannot fail to complete the eternal design of God. You have free choice and, if you can access it, great creative power at the Soul level. Most people simply do not access the potential that they have.

Thinking about it, where guidance comes from doesn't really matter, does it?

The point is whether guidance helps <u>you</u> in <u>your</u> purpose to learn and grow yourself. The books and teachings with which you become familiar and from which you benefit, have a message in them for <u>you</u>, and <u>you</u> brought them to yourself with the help of the other Souls with which you collaborate. A book that helps you may look very different to other people, and that's OK.

So, are you saying that other people actually see the book differently?

Every individual's interpretation of *anything* is highly personalized. The level of variation in something being considered by two individuals is affected by the subject (e.g. a concept or argument is highly variable whereas a physical object is less so) but there are always differences. The degree to which two individuals see or experience the same thing is driven by the context of the event in their lives and the shared (or otherwise) perspectives of the individuals such as cultural, educational and environmental backgrounds.

But can I (or anyone else) get answers from God?

Yes.

How?

By doing what you are doing. This is the very purpose of these exchanges, in fact.

Is that a cop out? How about if I demand to talk to God?

Would you believe us if we said "hold on – we'll put Him on the line"?

No, probably not.

Do you really need to hear from God?

It would convince me!

Of what?

That these dialogues are important and I should, well, listen to them.

Do you not listen to them?

Yes. They have changed my life.

OK then - God is talking to you without frightening you, making you think you're crazy, or risking others thinking you're crazy or a blasphemer.

I do believe that this is guidance from somewhere that I am comfortable with, and feels, well, *right*. And, frankly, I might well be scared if I really thought that "God" was talking to me...

Also remember what we told you earlier - everything you learn (and we show you) has to be within your own context and readiness. At this point, this method of learning, along with the books you are reading and researching is right for you.

Hang on though. Earlier on in this exchange you said that "God is everything and does not communicate His wishes because He does not have any. He has no needs, demands, opinions, rules or anything else. God just is." So, who spoke to all those who say they have heard Him, then?

They heard the voice that they needed to hear to answer their questions. The voice *was* God, at that moment, for each of them. And what they pass on to others is of God for all those that hear it and recognize its truths. God as an entity does not talk to you as such – He is not a human with human needs and habits.

God does not talk to us - that's big news, frankly.

Only if you interpret it as meaning God does not exist or care. That's not what we said. Let's be clear: God does not communicate with you directly like a person – because He is not a person. Another dichotomy – God does not communicate with you, but he does... through messengers like us.

So are you my "God" at this moment?

Listen, you don't need to hear from God, a "great powerful father", which is a mythical analogy that fulfills a human need for a parent figure. You, Simon, have heard from the true entity in ways that are meaningful to you. Remember we advised you before: *Attribute wisdom not to the speaker, but to your remembrance of what they said.* Apply this to everything you hear and read.

Yes, I remember that, but I guess things seem more convincing if they come from God Himself.

Yes, but only if you're looking for someone else to make up your mind, or choose for you. But it's you that has to choose differently. Even then, if you were to be given the answer by God in your own personal letter from Heaven, you would still have to make the choice yourself – and you'd still never be quite convinced it was actually from God, anyway...

That's true enough.

Review

1. God is not a human-like ruler who sits on a throne and sets rules and expectations, and decides who lives and dies like a king, queen or dictator:

    i.   God is the creator of everything that is, was, or ever will be. Our world is a tiny, momentary fragment within that

    ii.   God is everything, including us, and thus enables us to be

    iii. We live the human experience on God's behalf

    iv.   God does not communicate His wishes *because He does not have any*; He has no earthly needs, demands, opinions, rules or anything else

2. The parameters for your life are defined by your Soul, of which you are a single and temporary manifestation as it learns and expands to create and experience on behalf of God. You can choose what you want to be in relation to what you experience as that manifestation.

3. The experience of the same event or object witnessed by two individuals can vary dramatically: The level of variation depends on the subject (e.g. a concept or argument is more variable than a physical object), the context of the subject in each individuals' life up to that point, and the individuals' personal beliefs and perspectives.

CHAPTER 17

▼

At this point, the real world (or not real world as it turns out) seems a bit pointless.

It is real. For you, Simon Watson, this world is very real. And so it should be, and that is its purpose.

OK. But knowing that the reason for my existence, all the work and dreams and effort, is really for nothing more than a physical experience for my Soul, just makes me sad. And in the meantime everyone and everything just carries on, just the same.

Do you think that is because you believe people do not know what you know?

Yes, I guess so.

Everyone knows what you know; it's just that most choose not to remember. You are not responsible for them, only for yourself.

Are there lots of people like me?

Of course, many. Some are seeking proof and more data, just like you. Others have moved on with their new remembrance of the truth, or at least their level of understanding of it. Everyone is different and all are following the course they planned, as are you.

At my Soul level I planned everything to this point, even this exchange?

Your Soul planned it to a level of specificity sufficient for it to experience what it wanted to experience. As for the details and the potentialities, that's up to you, Simon.

So even these dialogues and my realizations to this point were to some level planned out. There's that puppet thing again. I really dislike that.

You will dislike it until you are willing to give up your own sense of specialness and self importance. It's like the moment when everyone accepted that the world is not the center of the universe, but just a satellite of the sun, and that the sun is one of many stars. Or when people learned that the world was round, not flat. There come times in our lives when we realize that something truly foundational to our beliefs is untrue, or has become that way because we have changed our minds. And it is often hard to accept.

Yes. Like the time I realized as a kid that my Mom and Dad really did not know everything and that they made mistakes just like everyone else.

An interesting and good example... The Gods of your world as a child turned out not to be Gods at all. And how did you feel when that happened?

I felt liberated... but also rather afraid.

Yes, indeed. You are like a puppet with his strings being cut, one at a time, as each old, supporting assumption is removed.

That's an interesting analogy. You're saying that to be free, a puppet has to break each and every string, in the knowledge that once he's done so he'll have to stand on his own two feet, or

perhaps just fall in a pile of wooden pieces. Mmmm... But where would that leave my Soul?

Do you think your Soul would want that to happen?

I've seen people fall into complete collapse and be wiped out. Or have heard of them, at least.

Do you actually know anyone, personally to whom this "wipe-out" has happened?

Well, no, come to think of it.

Think about that later.

OK, I will.

Now, back to these people you have "heard of". Did this happen to them because of their achievement of complete spiritual freedom and liberation?

No. More like their lives or families or finances got screwed up.

Yes, exactly. People's lives are affected in the way you mean due to worldly calamity - they do not free themselves spiritually but get totally tied up trying to fight for worldly matters and achievements. And in failing, they end up in dire straits - all tangled up.

We're off point again, I think. Where does that leave me, now?

Do you want to fight your way out of bondage, or are you seeking to free yourself, one string at a time, and grow the faith to believe that you will be able to stand independently when the last one is cut?

I see where you're going... but I get the feeling there's a fine line between the fighting and the faith approaches.   Does not the

cutting of each string become a fight, especially as you cut the ones that are holding you at crucial points?

Indeed. A challenge it is. You know that reaction you have whenever you hear someone say that you have to follow the teachings of the masters and leave behind what you have earned, learned, done and believed before?

Yes.

This is a core challenge. Your ability to step toward enlightenment hinges on your willingness to release this world as you have conceived of it to this point in every respect. Look up the parable in which Jesus says "Follow me".

OK. Luke 18:22: The parable of the rich man:

> 18 A certain ruler asked him, "Good teacher, what must I do to inherit eternal life?"
> 19 "Why do you call me good?" Jesus answered. "No one is good—except God alone.
> 20 You know the commandments: 'Do not commit adultery, do not murder, do not steal, do not give false testimony, honor your father and mother.'"
> 21 "All these I have kept since I was a boy," he said.
> 22 When Jesus heard this, he said to him, "You still lack one thing. Sell everything you have and give to the poor, and you will have treasure in heaven. Then come, follow me."

A few lines further on is the passage about the camel and the eye of the needle - one of your favorites, Simon, and one that has stuck with you since you were a boy. And there was a reason for that. In these words Jesus refers not only to money but to anything in which you have placed value, including beliefs, theories, data, knowledge and relationships. Note also that the "treasure in heaven" is instant upon surrendering all that stuff, not later. It comes at the moment you give everything up to follow Him.

But surely not everything! My most cherished things are people, my family.

You may think otherwise, but people are easier to surrender than your possessions or beliefs. For they have a will and life of their own and can sustain themselves. And as we have said before, they are also complicit in what happens to them, and your greatest gift to them is to enable them to be independent of you. When you release these things, as Jesus promised, you shall receive much greater reward, even in this life when you see that people and things return to you without your need of ownership, control or miserliness.   By giving them up, you receive them fully.

But this goes against everything that society tells us, and all common sense. It would be plain irresponsible to give everything up - not to mention lazy!

Giving things up and following a master does not mean abandoning worldly responsibilities. You see, there is a huge difference between a) believing and behaving in a way based on the assumption that loss of worldly things is failure and the end of you, and b) the ability to release those things, knowing they are of no real value. These are the same as beliefs in scarcity versus abundance.

Wait. What's the difference then? If I were to watch someone investing and saving and earning, how would I know if they were doing it from a position of freedom or one of grasping?

Does it really matter to you? If you have taken the step to relinquish, it matters not to you what others do. In the meantime, if it does matter (which means you are afraid), seek to know if they are doing those things from a position of love or fear, taking or giving back. It's about purpose not behavior. We have repeatedly said that you cannot DO anything in this world to gain enlightenment.

Ah - It's the being and doing thing again.

Yes. Do whatever you want in this world. You will do so based on your level of consciousness of what you truly are and want to be. By all means, do things that grant you wealth and worldly comforts. But when you see these as unreal, but most importantly as the things which you can GIVE AWAY to others (to whatever extent you are willing and able) then you will no longer be a slave to them.

OK. But when I see the folks going to Church, all I can think about is what I believe is their hypocrisy. I see churches as places generating money under false pretences.

Release the false obligation to show your strength and wisdom through judging others. Observe others, and listen to what I am teaching you, and just be what you are seeking to become. No-one else is wrong, no-one is offending God. Free yourself from your self-assumed responsibility to defend God and what is 'right'. Live your life as best you can. You have stirred to awaken and now recognize you are in a place that God is not, and therefore you cannot really be. Hear these calls to guide you home to the place you are seeking.

I will try.

OK.

But first, let's talk more about hypocrisy. The way I see it is that if people say one thing and then do another, they are hypocrites. If an organization says one thing and does another, then it is hypocritical. "Organized Religion" seems to me to be full of this, what with the huge money made and the priests that molest children and ministers that have affairs with their parishioners.

You already understand that there is nothing that you can do that will create enlightenment. *And if that is true, then it does not matter what others do, either, good or bad.* Instead of looking around you and seeing hypocrisy, disappointed you are not seeing goodness and truth, try looking at it differently. Try to see people who are genuinely creating the next highest version of themselves and realizing the desired experiences of their Souls, in collaboration with all others.

Hold on - I have a big question then. If people are only on an experiential mission for their Soul, then they, the human, cannot achieve enlightenment, can they? They themselves will not find salvation (or whatever they might call it) since they exist only as a brief experiential entity as part of a greater Soul. This is what Alan Watts meant when he described people as not being able to be anything but a "Quaking Mess" right?

What you just wrote was very important. Do you understand why?

Because if I accept it, it is the very reason that I need to be able to let go of my own specialness, the belief that all my efforts are to continue the existence of my ego, my identity as Simon Watson, in heaven after my death. In fact, I cannot achieve enlightenment at all, can I?

Go on.

If that's true, again I feel this is all pointless. Tell me - what's this life all about?

What do you think, now?

You sound like a consultant... It's about using this life to its fullest extent to define the next higher version of myself, based on what I believe that is. That belief is based on an overall objective set for me by my Soul, within which I have free will to act and develop in the ways I desire as a human. The level of consciousness of any human varies depending on the parameters of the mission their Soul set out, but also the amount of reconnection that the person makes with their Soul during the life experience. This is what you were explaining as the "bridge" between mind and Soul previously, and is my greatest exercise in free will.

Good! What you have just said is that Simon Watson cannot achieve enlightenment on earth, but he can live the highest version of himself there, and bridge back spiritually to his Soul, and thus toward God. I will add that it's a version of what Christianity describes as man being unable to go directly to God. What Jesus intended was to explain this bridge to you and show you how to cross it, but that got changed over time to Jesus himself being the sole bridge or intermediary, which was not his intention.

That's a significant explanation I will have to think about. In the meantime, this brings up free will again. Could someone go beyond the purpose and parameters set by the Soul? Let me have a go at answering that: No, the person cannot go past that since their very design and make-up, perhaps genetically, cannot conceive of such activities, right?

There is truth in your conclusion but there are also other complexities. A significant one is the influence of the collective consciousness of all other people and their combined creative power. This pushes individual people to the very limits of what it is they know, at their deepest physical and psychological levels, is their Soul's design. It is the cause of much stress in the system, and angst throughout human history.

What happens then - when people push those boundaries?

The more an individual pushes the boundaries of their true purpose (and therefore their conscious and subconscious identity), the more pressure he puts on himself, and the less 'at ease' he is. While you do have free will (for all the reasons we have discussed) the system also has a self-regulatory element to warn people when they are moving too far. This warning manifests to varying degrees - from a basic feeling of unease, to worry, depression and finally *dis*ease and illness.

Is that always what causes illness and disease?

Illness may be part of the experience chosen, and in the case of birth disabilities that is always the case. But most illnesses are the result of the dis-ease created in the way just described. But remember this: It is not about whether people are being good or bad. Dis-ease is created by a separation between a Soul's overall plan (which might be seen as good or bad) and its human entity's direction.

I guess all this is why some bad people don't seem to get the illnesses I think they deserve – they are following their course. Interesting - knowing this might make it easier to understand and forgive wrongdoers.

Wouldn't that be something?

What about death?

Death is always part of the normal process and Soul's plan: A Soul can achieve what it needs within a certain volume of experience and that may be in a short or a long life (in the way you define time). Whether this is attributable to any disease created by the individual is entirely circumstantial (and even convenient).

What about infectious diseases and epidemics and the like? Surely I cannot catch someone else's boundary-breaking?

This is what we meant by "other complexities", especially the collective conscious from which "infectious" diseases form. They are the result of mass dis-ease. Again, however, know that the results of these, including deaths, are part of the collaborative efforts of the Souls involved.

What about folks infected by people from totally different places, like the native peoples that were killed by diseases brought to them by invaders or traders? Those native peoples were not part of whatever boundary-breaking was being done by the newcomers.

These events were an infection on a large scale created by

globalization and have been given emotional power because of the apparent injustice. Remember, there is always a connection between everything - you need always to see the big picture, the grand plan of collaborative Souls. The viruses or germs that killed people with no immunity may have been brought there by a third party, but they were just the agent used to manifest a dis-ease already present in those affected.

This all sounds rather uncaring. Rather like it's just "tough" if you happen to be hurt by someone else.

That is a fair conclusion if you a) cannot accept that an overall plan is playing out, and that your experiences are part of that plan and b) continue to believe that that there are polarities like right and wrong, good and evil, winning and losing, living and dead. But if you can see that everything is only an experience, then it's not uncaring, it just is. All the while you label events with polarities, and identify one end of each as a right or wrong option you will continue to bounce between happiness and misery, perpetually caught up in trying to fix things, punish some and reward others. If you haven't noticed by now, reality is very different from what you thought it was. It's time to Observe.

I get the message that I should <u>stop</u> blaming and judging people. Apart from striving to Observe, what should I *start* doing?

Don't be hard on yourself! You have already started doing many new things. You are a very different person than you were. But your progress will be best helped now not by seeking more new things to do (although there are more, of course) but by stopping certain things that are blocking you. Put it another way, by letting go of old assumptions, habits and patterns you have had for your life so far. When you can do this, you will make way for new things. As Ruiz told you in The Voice of Knowledge, you have to retrieve some of the faith that you have invested in old beliefs in order to build anew.

Review

1. Our Souls plan our life possibilities. This is unpleasant to hear if we believe we are special, singularly important, and can become anything we want to be (the "American Dream" and all). But it's why most people's lives *are* relatively normal and predictable.

2. If your definition of success is tied to the external world (the fortunes of which are largely beyond your control) you will often (or eventually) consider yourself a loser or victim. Enlightenment or spirituality (or whatever you want to call it) enables you to free yourself from this - or at least traverse setbacks with greater speed and minimal distress.

3. Only when you can release material things and relationships can you receive them fully. This doesn't mean you have to throw everything away, but that you need to be *willing to do so*. Abundance and attraction are not all about *receiving* – they are about the reciprocal flow of energy.

4. Most people feel an obligation to show strength and wisdom (to self and others) by judging and correcting others. While such decisions are required to maintain our current societies through things like organizational and legal structures, imagine how much stress would be relieved in *your* life if you could stop doing what most people do – which is to judge and criticize and want to change *most* people, *most* of the time... Instead of taking freedom, <u>give</u> it.

CHAPTER 18

▼

After all this, I'm not clear about exactly what I am.

Take a shot at it.

OK, here goes. There is a Oneness that's all there is. The Oneness is "conscious", although not in the way we think of it in terms of a 'mind' or a 'personality'. For want of a better understanding, I'll say here that it is conscious in the sense that it is aware of itself. This awareness of itself creates a need for the Oneness to understand itself. Since the Oneness is all there is, it cannot understand itself in relation to anything else, so it creates things other than itself. Through these things, it observes what it is not, but since it created these things, these things are also what it is (or were before they became separate). In such a way the Oneness enables things to be, and could be considered *The Creator*.

The consciousness of the Oneness remains present in all the things it creates, through which the Oneness achieves the experiences it cannot have itself.

Thus it creates what I will call "Thinking Things". The Thinking Things exist together, all in the same space, and there is no separation. They are simultaneously environments (e.g. our universe) and their inhabitants, the former of which I will call "Dimensions", each of which has its own structures and rules.

Thus a Dimension itself has a purpose, awareness and desire to experience.

All of the Dimensions are also overlapping (since they occupy all that is) and the Thinking Things can participate in more than one Dimension at a time, or in the same Dimension, in multiple ways. To participate in a Dimension, they create or sponsor "Beings", each one independent, and these Beings exist as entities appropriate to that Dimension and its structure and rules.

In my "Universe" Dimension, most Beings are not aware they are literally just a part of a greater "Thinking Thing" (and therefore they're also unaware that they are part of the Oneness). This is necessary so that their experiences are realistic, independent and pure. However, they do have a general awareness of this truth, which creates the need for a God and the concepts of Souls.

Also in my Universe Dimension, Time is part of the structure and rules, so the Beings are subject to the experience of time as though time were as real as anything else in that Dimension. However, all the Dimensions are actually occurring simultaneously and there is no passing of time as such, so what Beings in the Universe Dimension experience as different historic periods are really occurring together, at once, in parallel. The Beings are separated by *perception*, not time. This is also true for space and distance, which are rules specific to the Universe Dimension.

A Being's *perception* is based on its Thinking Thing's initial design for it, but is changed by the experiences of the Being, including education, capability, personality, and experiences (i.e. interaction with the Universe and other Beings). This is part of what we tend to call "free will".

That said, the Beings vary in complexity. In the Universe Dimension, on Earth, they may be people or they may be a deer, an ant or a pebble. The more sentient the Being, the more its *perception* can develop away from its initially created state. This diversity is amplified by the Dimensions themselves, some of which may appear crude, relative to others. However, none are any less significant than others, since all provide the myriad of possibilities and experiences the Oneness wishes to create and experience through the Thinking Things.

In the Universe Dimension, *Human* Beings are aware of their link to their greater Thinking Thing to different degrees, usually considering it as being their Soul. However, they tend to think that their Soul is an eternal version of them or even a part of them, rather than knowing that they themselves are actually only one small (and temporary) part of a Thinking Thing. This may cause upset in those Beings who desire eternal life as the continuation of the mind of their current human form. But it need not, since it offers eternal life as part of something much greater.

That said, for highly evolved (or enlightened) Beings, eternal life can also be achieved in another way and the identity of the Being can become eternal in its own right: During their lives, humans who can understand the true nature of creation and bridge directly to their Thinking Thing, learn that the Universe is only one Dimension in which life, created by the Oneness, is constantly manifesting. Those who learn this can manipulate and create in the Universe Dimension in powerful ways, and may also be aware of other Beings and other Dimensions in which their sponsoring Thinking Thing is participating. They may even be able to participate in, or witness, other Dimensions and Being experiences, most easily during dreams, meditation or hallucinatory states. Ultimately, their minds may transcend from existing only in a temporary Human form, and they may become Thinking Things in their own right. This is the ascendance achieved by the true masters.

While all this could explain God as being the Oneness and the World as a place where many Thinking Things participate via billions of Beings (objects and creatures), this may not be the case. Instead, the World could be many Beings created by a *single* Thinking Thing, or, a even be a single Being, made up of parts which appear separate but are not... like the cell of a body which appears as a discrete entity, but only exists as part of something greater. The truth is probably somewhere in between, since boundaries are a concept forced on my thinking by the structure and rules of the Dimension in which I, Simon, exist. And in the end, it does not matter.

So I, Simon Watson, am a Being, a human... part of a bigger, Thinking Thing, to which I am trying to bridge back. And it is that bridging back to a Thinking Thing that I am working on, right now.

That's a very interesting way to describe things. Does it help?

Only if it's right.

Why does it have to be right?

That's a silly question. Sorry to be rude.

Alright, let's ask if it matters?

Of course it matters. I am trying to work out my very reason for existence here!

We are not saying it's unimportant. What we are suggesting is that at some point, once you've got things as clear as you can, you will have to make a decision - since you'll never get a perfect or correct answer, and will never understand, as a human, the huge complexity of the truth. But you can accept it, with "faith" as you might call it.

Why don't you just tell me straight?

We are, but we can only do so through you and your own lens, filters and readiness. Also, you need to realize that the "specialness" of this world cannot be disproved, for if it was, it would collapse. It has to remain apparently real and will always create just enough doubt of new evidence to disprove proof of its unreal nature. "That's its job" as you'd say.

Well, what the heck – make it collapse!

That's what we're doing for you here, but the collapse can only be in your perception and your experience of the world when you choose to see it differently.

So where does that leave me now?

Once you have got all this straight in your mind and you truly <u>believe</u> that you and the world are different, as Don Miguel Ruiz says you'll be able to rebuild your beliefs, claim back your faith, and begin life anew; you can claim what you know as the Toltec Naguals' "The Dream of Second Attention". When you are ready, you can begin to use this insight to see through this world and undo all the lies and assumptions that have driven your life to this point and you will do so with acceptance, not anger or judgment.

I guess it's the "leap of faith" thing, like you said.

When you can step to the edge and jump or just pitch forward into the possibilities, then you'll be there.

I see. So I'm on the right track then?

What you have now is a 'Personal Myth'[10].

But have I got the right answer?

You have something that works for you, at this moment. It will evolve with you. Remember that you cannot fail. And once you relax

---

10 Personal Myth: A sacred story that serves to explain and depersonalize your life; to shift you from unconscious participation in the routine world to conscious observation of your chosen life experience and purpose.

about time, and end your belief that you have to get this worked out soon, you'll feel better. You've already succeeded, remember?

So, if I've already succeeded, tell me again why I have to go through all this?

In asking that you show you've slipped back into the Simon Watson "Being" and forgotten you're a bigger "Thinking Thing". Stop worrying about Simon Watson and start enjoying life with knowledge of what it really is. Have fun. Live without fear. There are very few people who can do it. Try it.

Review

1. We cannot find perfect answers to our spiritual questions with human logic and thinking - unless we are willing to settle for ones defined by someone else (including those who claim that their answers come from God Him or Herself). At some point we will have to take a leap of faith – and that faith can be in our own knowing, or that of someone else.

2. The spiritual answers you develop will change over time and evolve with you. This may be disconcerting to people who desire stability and comfort - for them, the permanent solution of a defined religion with doctrines, rules and rituals is a great refuge.

3. Relax - you don't have to get all this worked out immediately - or before you receive eternal damnation for getting it wrong! You have already played your part for God, and He isn't waiting to punish you for making a wrong decision: That's just what people do to others – and themselves.

CHAPTER 19

▼

Back in our first dialogue, you said that sometimes I need a nudge from the universe to move on (although we have since clarified the universe is only one dimension, so I assume that the nudge comes from the Soul or "Thinking Thing" as I called it earlier). How does that work if every potentiality is playing out based on my free will?

Remember this dialogue has built and developed as it has gone along. Also remember that our explanations are limited at each step by your ability to understand and your lenses/interpretation.

OK, I trust you, so explain how that "builds" then...

The potential outcomes are influenced first of all by the design of your Soul's intended experience. So, since the Soul has an overall intention in its design for the experience, it can, and does influence certain outcomes in order to keep within the overall parameters of its design, especially at critical moments/events. It has mechanisms that indicate when parameters are being exceeded. Think of the Soul as a Prompter for a stage actor. Now, although such an intervention by the Soul will influence your Being's experience, the potentialities created should the Being NOT have responded to the Prompter can also be played out... if a Soul desires it.

Hold on there. You said CAN also play out... I thought they have already played out.

They all HAVE played out: But this is because there is no such thing as time. All potentialities desired by the Soul have occurred – there are some that have not yet played out, and may not. But, if the Soul wants to, then they will, and already have.

Are you just playing with words, here?

No, it's further explanation and a dichotomy. Everything has already played out, but it hasn't. Let us repeat: The "everything" here is more a function of the fact there is no time (things occur in a parallel) than one of completion of all potentialities in linear fashion.

Phew, that's hard to grasp, and I still feel that you're changing the game on me here. Let me try to clarify: Not everything has played out in terms of all possible events (potentialities), but it has all played out in the sense that those events that *have* occurred are all completed.

And should the other potentialities play out (i.e. the Soul chooses so) then those potentialities will also be complete, now.

OK: They have occurred because the potentiality presented itself and the Soul chose to explore it. And that, I guess, is creation.

As we said before, all this is a matter of volume of experience, not time. Using your Personal Myth, the evolution of the dimensions (of which your universe is one) is limited only by the expansion (of experience) or creativity, as you just said, of the Souls within them.

This makes me feel better – but I'm not sure why.

Perhaps because it somewhat lessens the discomfort you feel at each Being having to play out so many potentialities. This is not really a valid concern since the Beings always see their potentiality as singular and unique. Just as you do, now.

OK, but I have another question. This developing of answers links back to what you said in a recent conversation: "...You'll never get a perfect or correct answer and can never understand, as a human, the huge complexity of the truth." If that's true, am I just wasting my time here?

You cannot waste time since it does not exist. Since the alternative to time is experience, do you feel that what you have got in these dialogues and the reading and thinking you have been doing on this journey have been a waste of experience?

I'm not sure. Maybe I could say I could have been experiencing more "real human life", maybe working more, earning more money.

But you haven't chosen to do that other stuff, have you? And if you had, do you think you would have enjoyed that more?

No, but that's irrelevant since there's only now. Anyway, I have had an excellent time (sorry *experience*) over the last 12 months, with enough work to stay financially comfortable and lots of time for me, the family and these dialogues. I guess that answers my question.

Does it? Or are you asking a broader question? Are you asking that if you can never fully understand the truth, why bother to try?

Maybe I was, but when you put it like that, I think that I do want to try to understand - to the extent that I can. I think that a period in which I seek to understand all this (in my simple way) is an essential part of my purpose in this experience as Simon Watson.

OK.

Perhaps I am more concerned that these details are not exactly how it works – so my concern is less that I cannot understand the truth but that the answers you have given are just plain wrong or inaccurate.

The answers are as true as any others that you will find, but are true for you whereas others may not seem to be.

Are you avoiding the question?

We are trying to answer it. The truth is the Oneness: God. The Oneness is everything, including all the potentialities. And everything, including the Dimensions the Oneness creates, has potentialities.

Are you saying that there is not one answer to all this?

We are saying that it does not matter:

- At some point, once you've got things as clear as you can, you can make a decision to see things differently
- When you can step to the edge and jump into the possibilities, then you'll be there
- Once you relax about time, and end your belief that you have to get this worked out in a hurry, you'll feel better about it
- Stop worrying about Simon Watson and start enjoying life with knowledge of what it really is: Have fun
- Live without fear.

I hear you. And I have realized that I don't need to be in control or understand all of this, but in understanding what I can, I can develop toward that higher version of myself.

Review

1. The evolution of the omniverse (of which our u iverse is part) is limited only by the <u>creativity</u> of the Souls wit in it.

2. You cannot waste time because it does not exi .

3. See life as an ongoing opportunity to experie ce what you want to experience. Put another way, replace he well-used phrase "don't waste time", with "don't waste e *perience*".

4. Even if you can never fully understand the g ater truth of God, you should still seek to understand it as est you can; such investigation (regardless of level achiev d) is the life purpose of those genuinely seeking enlightenn ent.

CHAPTER 20

▼

OK. So I now have the liberation offered by the fact that there are no wrong answers. I now know that there are as many logical explanations for and models and myths of how everything works as can be thought up. Liberating indeed, but doesn't it make all this a bit meaningless? There seems to be no meaning in it all. It's just chaos, no order. As a human, don't I need meaning in order to carry on?

All we have shown you is that human life is not "meaningful" in the way that you previously thought about it. It's not that human existence is meaningless, but rather, it does not *need* a meaning. It's an experience with which you can create your own meaning. By the way - your Personal Myth for how everything works, the Beings, the Thinking Things etc. is as good as any, and works for you. You should continue to use it.

I'm glad that my myth is reasonable, but life still seems a bit meaningless... And that does seem to be a view that many of us humans have from time to time. Or perhaps "senseless": When we hear about what are called "senseless killings", for example. Yes, "senseless" - perhaps I feel that everything now, well, makes no sense.

Think again. Life is not meaningless in terms of it being without meaning or purpose. It has a purpose as we have discussed. And nothing is *senseless*. There is sense in every thing and creature in terms of both awareness and also a purpose or role in the big picture. What we are suggesting you do now is this: If you are looking for an answer for what is beyond your human being existence, let go of the need for everything to be ordered and logical and justifiable in human terms. The Oneness, as you called it, just is. God need not be justified or explained.

OK - So our human world and lives are meaningful and logical, but beyond that, the Oneness, is not?

Relax. Everything that God creates is meaningful. But you need not (and cannot) explain anything beyond earthly existence using human logic or measures (including ethical and moral judgments). Look up what you read by Gibran in *The Prophet*.

OK. Here:

> *And if you would know God, be not therefore a solver of riddles. Rather look about you and you shall see Him playing with your children.*
>
> *And look into space; you shall see Him walking in the clouds, outstretching His arms in the lightning and descending in rain. You shall see Him smiling in flowers, then rising and waving His hands in trees.*

That's a great and beautiful version of what you are telling me. I guess it is also a bit naïve for me to think that I can explain God, but I can't help but want to understand all this.

What God is to any one man or woman is highly personal to that individual. More importantly, the answer (which is only an idea) that anyone has about God is always correct – for them. And the information they need to build that idea is always forthcoming, and creates a way for them to connect back to their Soul... *in their own way, and their own time.* Your friend RC has many examples of how the information he needs just seems to 'turn up', as indeed, do you.

And thus you have had these dialogues and found the books and teachings you have.

I can go with that, for now, but I'll come back to it later. Here's another question: Yesterday, I was discussing our last conversation with RC. Out of that discussion, both of us were left, still, with a continuing lack of clarity about what we are. When I answered that question myself in a previous dialogue with you, I gave an answer which, as you have now explained is not right (or wrong). But that now leaves me again not knowing the finite answer - even if my myth is workable.

We are trying to explain that you don't need to know. Listen – here is a key for you: *You now know that all you need to know is what you are not, and that everything is no-thing. Thus, you need to know, nothing.*

"Nothing" seems to be a lot more important than I thought! *A Course in Miracles*, **states that we have "...too much faith in the body as a source of strength... "I need do nothing" is a statement of allegiance, a truly undivided loyalty. Believe it for just one instant and you will accomplish more than is given to a century of contemplation or struggle against temptation.**
... Make a place within you where the activity of the body ceases to demand attention. Into this place the Holy Spirit comes, and there abides. He will remain when you forget, and the body's activities return to occupy your conscious mind."

OK. Summarize what this means to you, now.

The body itself is the limitation, along with the mind and ego. One has to suspend commitment to it, even if in only a tiny part, in order to access the Holy Spirit and in doing so, that tiny space remains as your connection to beyond the human experience. It's that "bridge" between mind and Soul we have talked about. It is a refuge and place from which you can hear what you should be

doing. Thus, one changes from hearing only the ego, to hearing the Soul, and God.

Does that help you move on from yesterday's frustration?

Kind of... I am getting more comfortable with what all this means to my human life and how it can change it, but I am still not sure *what I am.*

State what you really want to know.

Alright, let me think. Here - What is the *human purpose*? **What's the purpose of all these millions of people, so many of whom are struggling and suffering?**

<u>Your</u> purpose is to live <u>your</u> life, as <u>you</u> see it and as <u>you</u> want to be, now.

There's that selfish thing again. But surely, that's not fair to all those people who don't have the great life I have.

What would be fair, then?

That everyone live a good and happy life.

How do you know what they need and desire? This is something you have understood already but maybe needs repeating here. You don't know what others desire, and, what they desire may be something that you don't like or understand. They may also have chosen at the Soul level to have what are, in your opinion, bad experiences. These experiences are relative and, if they are not yours, they are none of your concern. Unless you want them to be, in which case, you can get involved with them. It is your choice.

OK. So I should be selfish but am free to help others. But that does not answer my question.

Does it not? Your purpose is to live the experiences you have chosen, and if you want to, have fun doing it. You are lucky enough, right now, to know that your human existence is a brief embodiment of a fragment of your Soul, which itself was created by God to experience Himself. You're no longer lost in total belief of the singularity (and self importance) of your human existence. You can choose whether this makes you feel sad, small and pointless, or you can choose to see it as no more pointless than it was before - but now you need not take life so seriously. You can live without fear, and observe.

Oh. It's all about me being able to let go of this life, eh? It's just not important? I am just not important? That is very hard to hear.

Get out of the fear and self pity that your ego is creating here. Your human life is important to you, of course it is. But you just don't have to get so hung up on it. You're bigger than it, will outlast it, and have some great ideas about what that will be like. Use your Personal Myth. Believe it. It is AND WILL BE your reality.

OK. Let me think on that.

Alright, then.

In the meantime, another question: If I have chosen all this as my experience already (at a Soul level), have I not also chosen whether I am happy within it?

You have free will IN THIS INSTANT to choose a) How to receive it and b) What to do next[11]. Your purpose is to go on with this life, until it's over.

Mmmm... OK, one last question. Yesterday, RC asked about what creative powers we really have, if we are just this tiny experiential

---

11 I believe that this includes creating a different direction or outcome (presumably more to our liking) by using the spiritual and metaphysical solutions at our disposal.

blip. Specifically, what about wealth creation? What creative powers DO we humans really have here?

As he knows, creation can be seen as first thought, then word, then action. Until someone imagines the way in which they will create wealth and then turns it to word and action with a genuine belief that they already have what they are seeking (or it's on its way), they remain wanting. *Material* wealth is always created by a *material* action.

Perhaps that's the difference between want and desire then: Wanting is Desire without creative energy.

OK.

But what about a lottery winner, or an heir to a fortune, where was their work, then?

Those who allow their lives to be driven by others, by the collective consciousness, do not always have a bad experience. And you should not assume that such people have not worked to be where they are, in some way, or set up their circumstances at the "Thinking Thing" or Soul level as you would describe it.

But what if I, in my human mind, just can't imagine and therefore think of a way to create wealth?

Then you will not acquire it, of course. If you cannot imagine, then you cannot have the thought that will lead to action and creation. In your human life, these rules and logic prevail: Thought - Word - Action. But now you know how to access a place beyond this world. And as you evolve, you'll spend more consciousness there and what you consider "wealth", and what you desire, will be different.

So, getting stuff in the world takes worldly action, pure and simple. I had hoped that spiritual evolution would enable me to create wealth another way, I guess.

We have discussed ways to get what you desire in this world as part of your spiritual evolution. But that evolution changes your priorities. Let us say again, as you evolve, you'll spend more consciousness away from this world, and what you consider "wealth", and what you desire, will be different. So yes, you'll create wealth, but it'll be different.

That sounds like later on - what about me, <u>now</u>?

If you haven't noticed, your new thoughts and ideas are creating new words and actions and thus a new kind of wealth for you. Right now, in this instant, in this writing, because you BELIEVE and DESIRE it more than anything else.

I see, yes I do. I am "wealthier" now that I have ever been.

Review

1. We don't have to justify our lives with human achievement (be that fame, fortune, philanthropy or any other human achievement). God, and us, just are. God does not need not be justified or explained, and neither do you. What we achieve is a side product of being what we desire.

2. You need to discover that you are absolutely NOT what you are brought up to believe you are, and neither is anything else (or anyone) you see around you.

3. Your purpose is to live your life, as you see it and as you desire it to be, now. While you are doing that, realize you don't know what others desire at the Soul level - which may be something that you don't like, agree with or understand.

4. You have free will at any moment to choose a) How to receive that moment and b) What to do about it (including spiritual and metaphysical activities).

5. Material wealth is always created by a material action. But as you evolve spiritually, what you consider "wealth" will be different – and so will your actions be different.

CHAPTER 21

———————▼———————

I think I have realized what I have done here... I have seen how to wake up from the dream of life. I know of a truer reality, that I am not alone, I am eternal, and the influence and spirit of God is within me, and me a part of Him. I understand my purpose here - to experience life for God in the way I so desire.

Alright then.

But isn't this state of "grace" (for want of a better word for it) something that has to be earned and ratified by a church or a religious official of some kind?

You know you need no church approval. Grace cannot be granted or anointed by others. It is yours for the taking via your relationship with the truth. Look up the song, *Amazing Grace* on the internet.

OK. The whole song is highly relevant, but perhaps these two verses, which I did not know, reflect my learning the best:

> *Yes, when this flesh and heart shall fail,*
> *And mortal life shall cease;*
> *I shall possess, within the veil,*
> *A life of joy and peace.*

> *The earth shall soon dissolve like snow,*

The sun forbear to shine;
But God, who call'd me here below,
Will be forever mine.

Yes, indeed.

I want to go back to the previous conversation when you were explaining "The answer... that anyone has about God is always correct." Is there a difference, then, between every possibility being correct, and <u>nothing</u> being correct?

Clarify what you mean.

What I mean is if it does not matter if something is correct or incorrect, then NOTHING MATTERS at all, right?

Again: *All you need to know is what you are not, and that everything is no-thing. Thus, you need to know, nothing.*

Change your perspective - It depends on how you hear the statement "Nothing Matters". You can hear it negatively or positively. What we are telling you is that nothing really <u>does</u> matter – it's all you need to know.

But surely God matters?

Nothing does matter - but it is still nothing. You continue to seek for right and wrong, but whether something matters (or is matter) is a condition relevant only to the <u>human</u> world. But God *is not* matter and does not *need to* matter. God just is.

So what is He then? Nothing?

God is the only constant; He cannot be explained by human logic, although you have needed to come to this point in your journey by using logic. Think of it this way: Logic is just a path of knowing on which you can walk and move from one human perspective to another. It is a winding mountain path, up which you walk as you ascend to the highest version of yourself. At the peak is a moment of faith where the path of logic falls away and you step out into *nothing and not knowing*. And there, you find the truth. You cannot know the truth, be given it, buy it, learn it or make it. You cannot describe it or write it. You can only experience and feel it. And only the truth is peace[12].

I do feel it, but won't there always be a question, nagging away in the back of my mind? I do feel that I have created that space inside me that *A Course in Miracles* talks about. I can now find it when I want to, and it does quiet the storm of the world. I can turn away from immersion in the world and cease to let it concern me as something I have to control. The world does, in those moments, seem to be something that's just happening and I am a tiny part and observer of it. But will I ever completely take the leap off the path of logic?

This may surprise you, Simon… but you already have. Your remaining sense of fear is not about making that decision; *it's in wondering where you'll fly and where you will land*. And when you do, there will be no doubt left.

Wow. Yes, I guess I have made that decision, after all this. Do I no longer need logic, then?

In your human life, of course you will. But beyond that, you need to *not know*; to stop needing to prove and explain everything in human terms. You do not need human logic in your spiritual evolution unless you become afraid and try to cling to the plants and branches of the mountainside, to end your flight, and climb back onto the path. And many do.

I'm going to be tempted to do that a lot, right?

---

12 What is meant by "peace" in these dialogues is of great importance - as you will see later in this book.

Your ego mind and body will do all it can to return you to the mountain. But now you can fly. Now you can find out what comes beyond the world and its rules and logic.

Review

1. The question as to whether something matters (or is solid matter) is relevant only to our world and universe. God, who is beyond our universe, is not matter and has no need to matter (both of which are conditions in our universe).

2. God is the only constant; He cannot be explained by human logic which can only take you so far in understanding greater spiritual truth – eventually you have to be OK *not* knowing.

3. "You cannot know the truth, be given it, buy it, learn it or make it. You cannot describe it or write it. You can only experience and feel it. "

CHAPTER 22

▼

I have recently read a suggestion that many religions originate from a separate, overseeing consciousness – one which deliberately seduces humans into lives of materialism, power, infighting and oppression. It made a big impact on me for some reason. What can you tell me about that?

Do you think it's true?

It does seem to reflect what I see in the world.

Is it what you believe?

I do observe the suggested unpleasant human behaviors, but the suggestion here is that those behaviors stem from a consciousness which has <u>actively driven</u> humans in that direction. This seems to go counter to our previous discussions.

In what way?

Well, using my myth, it would imply that at least one "Thinking Thing" is, well, "evil" in that it's making humans that way.

What is your point or question?

I guess I assumed that the "Thinking Things" or Souls are, well, neutral. But the above statement implies a deliberate and evil manipulation of Beings... which would make the Soul itself evil, right?

The Soul, as you call it, can plan and initiate any experience in what you call a "Dimension". It's what we said before. From your perspective, you can decide if the experience was one which was evil or good. Or you can let theorists and religionists make that determination for you.

So, Souls just want an experience, and that might be good or bad depending on my perspective. Yes, OK, that is what you said all along. So now you're saying that the above statement simply means that a consciousness at my "Thinking Thing" level has *chosen* to create experiences based on materialism and oppression.

Does that make sense?

Yes it does. But are some Souls inclined to create more of what I might consider bad experiences than others?

They can create whatever they want.

That's not an answer to my question. Do some Souls choose to be, or turn out to be, evil?

Your question is based on the flawed concept that an entity such as a Soul could become more or less good through amassing a volume of experiences of one type (good or bad) over *time* and could be assessed as such at a certain point in time. Remember, there is no time. Everything happens at the same time, and as such is always in balance. Experiences of all types happen all together but as we have explained, as a human being you experience only the potentiality you're in at a certain moment in your perceived time.

So Souls can't become evil since there is no "becoming" for them to do? They are already complete, as it were, and that's a balance?

No, they do become or evolve through the experiences they choose to create – and this is the constant growth or expansion we have talked about. However, what <u>you</u> feel as good or bad exists only in your human perception. You cannot judge them.

So wait a minute. Even if there is no time, could not a Soul just create a lot of bad experiences first, and therefore be considered bad at that moment? Or perhaps one could get a taste for the bad stuff and stick with it?

There is no time so nothing is created first - or in any such linear order. Think about your question a bit more and focus it.

OK. Are there Souls who create more bad than good experiences and therefore are "bad angels" or "demons", as it were? I am back to worrying about whether evil is an entity, and even if that entity opposes God.

By the fact that you and others have imagined this possibility, it is one which can and has been played out - in human terms in the human experience.

But what is the <u>truth</u>? I don't want to know what might be, but what is! Beyond just me.

God is. God is all there is.

You're still not answering my question! Are there bad Souls, or demons, or whatever, out to destroy the earth and God?

Ah. There's your real question. There is, in your dimension as you call it, anything and everything you can imagine from within your human mind, including its apparent destruction. But it's not relevant outside your dimension, which is just one of many. Fears of demons and loss and destruction in your mind are based on the rules and paradigms relevant only to your dimension. Once outside it, the whole purpose and nature of everything is different. Until you can accept that what is beyond your world is not comparable or explainable in your terms, you will remain frightened.

Sorry to be a pain – But are there good and bad Souls, or not?

There are Souls. And they are all doing lots of things. And I cannot explain or justify their motives to you since they are, literally, not of your world. But they do participate in it in the ways we have explained. And you are part of them.

OK then – are some Souls against God? Wanting to destroy Him?

You're not listening. The desire to destroy anything is something relevant to your human world/universe Dimension. Beyond that, destruction and winning and losing are just not relevant.

So other dimensions don't have this tendency for evildoing then?

We cannot explain other dimensions to you. They would make no sense to you. Even those that are similar to your dimension would not comprehend your judgment of good or bad, right or wrong. This happens even in your world - think of a lion killing and eating an antelope. To you, the act looks bad, but to the animals, it just is. What we mean is that what you regard as good and evil would be considered nothing or even an opposite by an observer from another dimension. Most importantly, you need to understand that beyond the many dimensions, at the source, the Oneness, there is no judgment, only creativity.

So why do we do this destructive stuff here, then?

Because you can. And because you can, you provide the relativity of what is not God, so that God can experience Himself.

So we're God's fall guys then?

That's an interesting way to look at it. Remember that the only relevant person here is you – do you feel like God's fall guy?

No. But I think others would say yes!

Your purpose here is only your own. What you now know should show you *your own truth.*

Alright, then. So what I am understanding is that all stories that good and evil are at war are solely a result of humankind's assumption that what is beyond this world has the same flaws as us – those being to hurt and exploit one another in some way. The truth is that beyond this Dimension the rules are totally different.

That's a fair summary. But hurting and exploiting are not flaws; they are elements of your chosen experience.

Hold on. If I accept that good and evil things are just relevant to us here, does that answer my question about whether there is a consciousness which is actively pushing bad stuff on humankind?

Listen: *There is no malevolent consciousness whose purpose is to make your life miserable.* There are Souls who are creating experiences which you interpret and influence in ways we have discussed.

OK, but there's a related thing that came up too: That entities from other dimensions are interfering with our world (that's what some folks call "UFOs"). Can you tell me if that's true?

As we explained, Souls can participate in more than one dimension at a time. It is possible for dimensions to be "short-circuited" by Souls and thusly interference can take place across dimensions. At those moments, the potentiality visited has additional possibilities, sometimes seeming positive and sometimes, negative.

So that's a yes then! But the thought of interference of a negative kind from another dimension is not only bizarre, but positively frightening.

You need not be afraid. Nothing of the greater truths you have learned has changed. Continue to apply your learning, and do not get sucked back into the game, however bizarre or alarming the temptations may be.

OK, I'll stay centered. But hey - there really <u>are</u> such things as entities from other dimensions or UFOs, then?

You knew that already – you saw one in 1997.

I don't know what I saw that day...

You witnessed two dimensions pressing against one another - like a finger pressed into the skin of a balloon, seen from the inside of the balloon. Events such as these are many and varied and have different purposes and causes. In your case, it enabled you to be more open minded – to accept that what many consider just stories may sometimes be true.

That's exactly what it looked like – getting bigger and smaller and then just disappearing! Was that event put there just for me to witness?

Again, <u>you</u> are all that matters in <u>your</u> experience. Everything is put on for you, while it is simultaneously put on for everyone else – who are also you related in the ways we have described.

Whew, that's hard to get my head around. But I want to go back to something you said earlier in this dialogue – you said that at

the core, the Oneness is "only creativity". Why did you not say "Love" or "Goodness"?

Because the truth is, it is only <u>creativity</u>. And as part of creativity, there are not only new beginnings and growth but also endings and change. *But there is no malevolence*, just constant creation and recreation. Look at it this way: The nature (the geography, the flora and fauna) of your world represents this truth – it is what is meant by God's creation of the Earth. In nature there is life, and death, growth and decay all together, seamless, and it just is, peaceful and accepting amid even powerful natural upheavals and turmoil. This is God. He loves it all - not because it is "good" but because it is Him.

Review

1. In our universe, anything and everything we can imagine from within our human minds, including the universe's complete destruction, is a potentiality. But 'destruction' in the way we know and fear it is not relevant <u>outside</u> our dimension/ universe where good and bad, winning and losing and our other such polarities are not relevant.

2. Once we can accept that what is beyond our world is not comparable or explainable in our terms and that our human 'evils' do not extend beyond our own mind, we can stop being frightened – and end our reliance on the generosity of God (or more directly religions) to give us an eternal and happy life after this nasty one.

3. At the micro level, the actions of people hurting and exploiting each other are elements of their chosen experiences, in the same way as they might be helping and supporting each other. And at the macro level, there is no malevolent consciousness making life miserable for some, and neither is a good one making things wonderful for others.

4. God is <u>creativity</u>. And creativity has endings and change as well as new beginnings and growth. But there is no malevolence, just constant creation and recreation.

CHAPTER 23

▼

I have learned from various sources that the world I see is a projection of my own thoughts and beliefs. How literal is that?

Firstly, let us remind you that explanations of what is outside your human experience and perceptions are limited in their accuracy by the fact that they use logic and principles applicable to only your own Dimension. They are therefore more of an analogy than a fact.

OK. But these analogies help me understand and feel better. I guess I need to let go of needing to understand everything.

Yes, but don't throw the baby out with the bathwater, as you would say. For the time being, you are here in your dimension as a Human, and you have to use the capacities you have here. It's not a matter of these explanations being of no use, but understanding that you need not, and cannot, get a complete and perfect answer.

OK.

These explanations and the conclusions you reach provide you with a bridge to greater understanding while you remain in your Dimension. But do not undervalue them. While in this dimension, in your current consciousness, this is the only way that you can comprehend what you are learning. It is no more a weakness than using verbal or written human language day to day – with which communication is quite limited.

I understand. I accept the limitations imposed by my participation in this Dimension. But is there any way to get around these limitations while I am alive, then?

As you have learned, altered states of consciousness can be and are attained in many ways – From meditation and sleep, to near death experiences and psychedelic drugs.

Interesting – use of psychedelic drugs to escape the current dimension - that's what Thaddeus Golas referenced in *The Lazy Man's Guide to Enlightenment*, and recently a friend of mine shared his own such experiences.

Political correctness and laws and 'wars' against drugs don't change what they are.

But let's get back to my question: How literal is your statement that the world I see is a projection of my own thoughts and beliefs?

The world around you is happening, and you are part of it. It is very complex and integrated. It is God's plan and you play within it.

That sounds like I have no influence on it at all!

If you mean you don't drive it or control it, then that's true. What you do, as we have explained, is to respond to it. That's your free will. Beings with a level of spiritual awareness will behave based on what they see and experience from a place of understanding that the world is not all there is, or what it appears to be. Others, those without awareness (the Players), go along with the plan, fully believing that they are single and independent entities.

Again I feel that I am a pawn. Sorry to go over old ground, but again, what kind of freedom do I really have?

The need for control is your major blockage. Listen: Your freedom (or "free will") is not in your ability to control the world. Those who think they can are really delusional prisoners. Even the greatest historical figures influenced a part of the world for a miniscule moment in time (as you perceive it). Your true freedom, that to which you are awakening, is your ability to remove yourself from immersion in the world, and make choices that define the highest version of yourself you can imagine, describe, and put into action – *within the world you perceive.*

That's an important thing, right? This is not about gaining anything which will give me power or control here. But how does that relate to my question?

The world is there, and like God, it just is. Even the things within it that you can directly claim to have created or caused to come about, are parts of the world which are there with, or without you.

Hold on. If I built a house, it would not be there without me.

If you built a house, it is there, now. And as you know, there is only now. If you were to be gone the next instant, the house would still be there. There is only now, and that which you see about you is there, whether or not you had anything to do with it.

Phew, that's a bit heavy. This issue of there only being now is a big key isn't it? I mean, what I have just learned is that because that is true, I really don't matter - my legacy or future - because the world just is, right now, with or without me. Oddly, that feels freeing.

But do you understand what we said? It is a milestone in your understanding.

I think so.

Alright, let's continue. When we say that the world you see is a projection of your own thoughts and beliefs, we refer to your *interpretation* of it: Your perspective of what it is, and what it means. The world only exists for you, in that way. You can look at an object and see it as good or bad, big or small, pretty or ugly. It's your interpretation and perspective at that moment, and at that moment, that is what it IS. Whenever you see an object or event, it requires you to interpret and judge it, from your current perspective – which includes all the knowledge, beliefs and assumptions you have built up to that point. Thus as you observe the world, THAT is what you see, so that is what it IS, until such a time as you choose to see it differently. What other people see may not be the same – they will see, and therefore it will be, what it means to them.

So, when you say "the world you (I) see" you mean my interpretation of it, not what it actually is in terms of physical objects and events.

Yes and no. What you need to understand is that since you are all that matters in your experience here, *your interpretation is more relevant and real than the physical object itself.* It is in this way, and by fully accepting this, that miracles occur – that is how mountains are moved. That is pure faith. We have mentioned before that only advanced Beings or Masters can influence the world against collective consciousness (collective consciousness is what makes the world what it is in most people's experience). We can now add that such Beings have faith strong enough that their perceptions and interpretations can be imparted to others so that physical matter changes for everyone - since everyone now interprets it in the way of the Master.

So the "simple" answer to my question is this… My world is here, it just is, and only has meaning based on how I perceive and interpret it. I can influence it therefore by changing my perspectives, perceptions and beliefs. And in doing so, I can change my world - because I am now interacting with it in a different way, even though materially, it has not changed. However, those who

have sufficient faith in their beliefs and perceptions can influence those of others to the extent that, to all intents and purposes, the physical world actually changes - because everyone sees it the new way.

That is a fair summary.

But that summary sounds like nothing new when I put it that way, but I feel what you walked me through to get there was very significant.

We intend that our explanations help you understand and then <u>believe</u> what you already know.

Review

1. Even if we can never fully understand the greater truth of God, our human minds are the only way we can comprehend what we are learning about Him. Supplement your logical thinking with ways to create additional/enhanced states of consciousness and communication methods.

2. Your "free will" is not an ability or duty to change or control the world. Even the greatest figures in human history influenced a <u>part</u> of the world for a <u>blip</u> in our universe's time. Your free will is to make choices that define and create the highest version of yourself you can imagine, within the world as you perceive it.

3. Whatever you do or create is there, now. Once it's there, it's there... whether or not you had anything to do with it. That means that neither your legacy nor your future (i.e. what most people spend their lives getting hung up about) really matter because the world just is, right now, with or without you. That can be freeing or terrifying... depending on your level of acceptance that your life is not of singular time-bound importance, but actually a contribution to a greater, timeless whole which exists only in the now.

CHAPTER 24

─────────▼─────────

I have been reading about Gnosticism which seems to have a lot of principles which fit for me. Yet it brings up yet more questions. I am again torn about whether there is one better "religion" to follow than others.

There are many ways to God.

But are some wrong?

None are wrong. Errors are made by man and are unavoidable since man cannot understand the complexity of the truth.

Why do I continue to search, then?

Because you do - It is where you are. It was no coincidence that you re-opened *A Course in Miracles* at the same time you began to look into Gnosticism.

Indeed. The course states "...there is need for help beyond yourself as you are circumscribed by false beliefs of your Identity. ...Help is given you in many forms, though upon the altar, they are one... But they have names, which differ for a time, for time needs symbols, being itself unreal. God does not help because he knows no need. But he creates all helpers of his Son while he believes his fantasies are true. Thank God for them, for they will lead you

home." That is quite clear: There are many ways, all provided by God.

You too have created many clear answers in these dialogues. But they will only be whole and permanent for you when you can release your conviction that your world is the single reality and believe that what you are learning here is a path to the truth that will set you free. While you are searching you cannot find, because it is only when searching ends, that finding becomes.

But I have to search *in order* to find!

You HAVE found. Now, you have to be, and believe, and the truth will be there for you. Just live your new truth; love life with the acceptance of that truth.

That sounds lazy or arrogant, actually.

In relation to what? Is that a judgment you would make of yourself, or one you assume would be made of you by others?

Both. I guess I have been programmed with the fact I am not worthy and need "continual improvement".

What you are now seeking is real growth, real progress. Progress in your material world is unreal and of the ego. Simon, you must now accept that true growth is not achieved in the same way as it is in the human world.

Why not?

You cannot search for anything real in the world because it is not the finite reality you thought it was, and you search the world using the eyes and the mind – limited to interpretations and perspectives of the ego.

Again I will reference *A Course in Miracles*: "Knowledge is not the remedy for false perception… The one correction possible for false perception must be true perception. [But even] it will not endure. But, for the time it lasts it comes to heal. For true perception is a remedy with many names: Forgiveness, salvation, Atonement, true perception, are all one. They are the one beginning, with the end to lead to Oneness far beyond themselves. True perception is the means by which the world is saved from sin, for sin does not exist. And it is this which true perception sees."

If reading such words from *A Course in Miracles* or any other source helps you, then they are right and valid, just as those of any other sources that move you forward, just as we seek to do. Use all of them. As we said before - listen to all of them, judge none of them.

But I have this nagging feeling that there must be a right religion or philosophy out there somewhere, and all this work with you is just guiding me to it.

That will be true, if that is what you truly desire. For many, that is their truth and goal. Is that what you truly desire?

No. Actually, as I was writing my last statement, I felt that I already know that. This is my journey. Perhaps I am just afraid that someone will think me a liar or blasphemer or the like.

If you wish to seek answers, don't let fear of needing to be right or approved-of influence you. And just as importantly, don't seek to create a case for convincing others they are wrong. Just find your own truths and others will be drawn to them, if they so desire.

OK. This makes sense. I do tend to want to find the right answer, and part of that will be that someone else will say "yes, that's correct, you're saved". Perhaps I need God to say that.

We hope you already know there is no "saving" to be done - except freeing yourself from being lost in the illusion. And do you think that any judgment by a Human Being has any relevance to God?

No, in fact I'm embarrassed to have suggested that.

Well, cease to be embarrassed. There is no such thing where there is no judgment, superiority, or fear. In such moments of awareness accept peace, not embarrassment.

OK. Can I just ask about Gnostic theory and my 'Personal Myth'?

Certainly... as long as you remember that it does not matter.

Agh... Just let me get it out of my system, OK?

Go ahead.

I have read that Gnostics (at least some of them - they seem quite variable) consider that the God of the Old Testament is a demigod, the "demiurge", who created the world. He's a subordinate to the Oneness or to some extent, even a rebel. And a jealous and cruel rebel, at that!

That is what you have understood. Go on.

Well, part of my myth was that the Dimensions are conscious as they are also the "Thinking Things". Could it be that the demiurge is the consciousness of my Dimension?

Does that help explain the theory of the demiurge in your terms?

Yes.

And does using your myth make the demiurge seem less frightening and more a part of the structure that the Oneness intends?

Well, yes again.

Then it is serving its purpose.

But we said that Thinking Things are not evil, just experiencing. Could a Dimension be evil, then?

So if the demiurge did things which you would consider bad, like being jealous or arrogant, do you think that would make it totally evil?

I guess not. It's just being, and since it's not the Oneness, then nothing it does is inherently anything - it's just experiencing everything. In fact, that might explain why biblical scriptures seem to have a God which is in one moment cruel and in another, good. Yes - that would explain a lot! It's not the Oneness involved here, but a consciousness of Its creation! The demiurge thing makes a lot of sense. Is that right?

Does it help you?

You're not going to give me a definitive answer, are you?

No. And it would make little difference if we did. It is still your choice. Again we tell you, take what you have just learned and seek to use it to see the world differently. You cannot free yourself from the world by seeking to disprove it by using its own artifacts.

Once more I will reference A Course in Miracles: "What is the ego? Nothingness but in a form which seems like something. In a world of form, the ego cannot be denied, for it alone seems real.... Who[ever] asks you to define the ego and explain how it arose can be but he who thinks it is real and seeks by definition to ensure that its illusive nature is concealed behind the words that seem to make it so. There is no definition of a lie that serves to make it true." The course uses complex language, but the point is that we can't make something true by the act or result of explaining it.

Review

1. There are many ways to spiritual enlightenment and God – and since <u>everything</u> is of God, so must ALL of those ways have been provided by Him. Therefore we must conclude that none are wrong and he is OK with all of them.

2. Accept the lessons you feel are true - and then stop searching. Do this because if you continue to search you never use what you found. In accepting, you open yourself up to new and enhanced truths which will come to you without struggle.

3. There's no need to seek approval for what you believe about spiritual truth. And don't seek to create a case for convincing others you are right; just find you own truths and others will be drawn to them, if they so desire.

CHAPTER 25

▼

There's a (crude) saying I heard once – it said "Eat shit – a trillion flies can't all be wrong". At this point in our exchanges I have a sense that maybe I am wrong with all this, and what I am writing here. So many people, for so long, have had their own ideas and theories – why should I think I know better?

There are many kinds of flies. They eat many things.

Yes, but they seem to agree that excrement is acceptable.

Perhaps you are giving excrement more credit than it deserves. Flies enjoy a wide variety of food options, more than you, actually. You only consider excrement as relevant here because you don't like it.

Maybe I have not made my point.

No, you have made it and we answered it.

I need more help, then. This is about spirituality and religions – a lot of people like them, right? And I am saying that if so many other people have accepted a theory or religion, why would not one of them be correct? And that would make me, and all this, wrong!

As we have said, they are all OK.

But many religions profess to be the only way to salvation, and indeed, that any other religions are not only wrong but following them will mean their followers' damnation.

So what's your point here? Are you asking if you'll be damned to eternal hellfire if you don't choose one of the mainstream religions?

Yes, I guess I am.

Do you want hellfire to be in your experience?

No, of course not!

OK then.   Desiring it is the only way that will be in your experience.

Come back to my question... Will I be damned if I make the wrong choice?

Who will damn you?

God, of course.

Do you still believe in "God" in the same way you did before you started these dialogues? That there is an all-powerful God who is vengeful and jealous and who has spent effort preparing endless flames and tortures for the majority of mankind's Souls?

Well, no, come to think of it. The "Oneness" as I called it, is not evil. It just is, right?

Do you think the Oneness as you called it would damn you for eternity if you didn't choose the right *church*?

No, that would make no sense. But perhaps my Soul or Thinking Thing or a Demiurge would...

Are *you* your Soul?

I'm a part of it.

Then if you were to experience hell, who would be making that choice?

My Soul...which I guess is me, or the greater version of me. But suppose that's what my Soul *does* intend? I'm afraid about that — my Soul may choose a horrible next experience for me!

As we have said, a Soul can set the parameters for a Being to experience whatever the Soul so desires. But you must know this: Firstly, your current Being's consciousness, Simon Watson, will not experience it. Second, the Human Being who does experience such a life will consider him or herself as original as you consider yourself, and its experiences will *not* be relative to yours. That is why you, Simon, must focus on your life.

Let me say this, then: You're trying to tell me that I just have to live this experience. I must stop worrying about what's next since it will be something which will not be experienced by consciousness of which I am aware, here, as Simon Watson.

Does that make sense to you?

Yes, but now I feel that I will truly "die" when my human Being dies, whereas I hoped I would continue in some way. That's my ego doing its job again, eh?

You will continue, but not as Simon Watson. Be not afraid to give up this "Human Beingness", for you will become aware of your true nature when you die, and as part of something greater, you will choose another experience and will live that experience fully and with conviction. The words of Jane Roberts in *Seth Speaks* give excellent outlines of the possibilities and alternative realities that will be available to you, even though your understanding of Seth's descriptions is limited by human language. Your concept of a single step between Soul/Thinking Thing and Human is effective, but extremely simplistic. There is a huge and ever changing arrangement of alternative realities in which you will participate next. Jane Roberts' book will help you.

Since there is no time, I have already lived the other lives and existences, right?

Avoid using the past tense. Nothing has ended - you are *still* living them. Don't see them as complete – they are happening. In each and every happening/potentiality the birth, life, and death you experience as finite is happening simultaneously.

So all this is about me accepting that what I am experiencing, here as Simon, is just a little piece of the real me. And I have a level of understanding of that truth in a way that some others do not. And that understanding means I can live my life (and see the world) differently, if I so choose. Sorry to keep repeating myself and going over old ground, but this is hard to absorb.

Indeed. Other people, and all their religions, are ways in which Beings are seeking to obtain a sense of liberation from the world which, to some degree, they know is not real. You are all searching for the same thing, in your own ways.

Will we ever find it?

Everyone already has. You just don't know it or believe it as the being called Simon Watson - yet.

It's just very hard to consider that the "I" that I know will be gone, and that I will not be able to continue with the same singular awareness and identity.

The fact is you won't want to! When you are through with this life, you'll leap into the truth with relief and excitement. You may be pacified by the fact that the 'greater you' will not forget the experiences of Simon Watson, because they will be there *within* the greater you and you will be able to remember and, as Seth explained, re-live them at will, seeing through all the possibilities you so desire.

It's really mind-boggling to think that at some level I am living all the possibilities, yet to me here, right now, this potentiality seems so real, so finite. I cannot decide if that feels liberating or frustrating.

People respond very differently to this realization (in whatever way they get to it). They may find it a good thing or a bad thing. They may use it to seek liberation and joy, or hide themselves away in a religion which provides a myth that they can live with, and choose doctrines and orthodoxy that remove their need to think about this any further.

That makes a lot of sense – I <u>am</u> getting an urge to seek a religion on which to hang all this: Hence my questions about Gnosticism. It's also why I like *A Course in Miracles* which does not seem to be tied to any specific religion. I guess I'm feeling the temptation to get sucked back into the game that you mentioned before.

OK.

But why would people commit themselves to a religion, and then either create or support claims that their religion is the <u>only</u> truth - and that any others are blasphemous?

Those who are comfortable with their truth and use a religion to reduce the complexity of thought that true awareness of reality creates do not always condemn other religions. You can see this in the levels of diversity and acceptance in some religious groups. Others however, believe that a willingness to fight for their religion is required in order for them to demonstrate their conviction - and thusly gain the stability and safety they seek from it.

Yes, I understand that. It just seems a shame that in doing so they can go against the very essence of their religion!

Your concern with that is based on your own judgmental perspective of abhorring hypocrisy. Here is something to think about: *To cry "hypocrisy!" is merely to demonstrate that you are blind to another person's perspective or predicament.*

I'll think about that! I have another question: You said that some people use a religion to reduce the complexity of thought that awareness of reality can create. This seems like a very good reason to choose and follow a religion - one that might work for me.

Why would that work for you?

Because if I were to know the truth, but simplify my life and mind by aligning with a religion which is basically in line with that truth yet which is tolerant of others, that might be OK with me.

The choice is yours. But whichever route you choose, your last statement is a realization that will help intolerance of traditionally religious people. You do not know what others truly believe. As we just said, perhaps it's time to demonstrate that you can accept other people's perspectives and predicaments, and that seeing hypocrisy is just another name for judging others and projecting guilt and frustration away from yourself.

I hear you.

Review

1. When you die, you will become aware of your true nature; a part of something greater, your Soul, and a contributor to God.

2. When your human experience is done (whatever it was, grand or small) your greater self (your Soul) will remember it, and place it with that of all its other myriad of existences. As part of your Soul, you return to your Soul consciousness. It is in *that* way that you live forever.

3. You do not know what others truly believe. If you can accept other people's perspectives (often created by their problems and predicaments) and resist the temptation to judge them, you will begin to recognize that you are only projecting guilt and frustration away from yourself.

CHAPTER 26

▼

I am feeling stressed and a bit astray. How am I doing – or should I say "being"?

There is no judgment of what you are doing or being. There just is you, here, now. And you can choose to observe that - just as you are now.

I keep judging myself all the time. Judging and doing too little observing.

You <u>are</u> observing - and as you learned recently from Pema Chodron's teachings, you are observing yourself and your "Shenpas", most of the time.

I like the Tibetan word shenpa (Tib. *zhen pa***) - which I would describe as the urge within us to react (usually with negative results) to something based on strong, probably subconscious feelings or beliefs. I have been caught up in my shenpas the last few days; a bit disappointing, really.**

You are hard on yourself. You have made great progress simply by being aware and recognizing your shenpas as you go about your business. That is the first and most significant step. You are aware almost 100% of the time now.

I know I need to stop all this judging, right?

You have to make material judgments all the time – when you drive, pick up a cup, or take any physical action or decision in order to function on the material world as you perceive it.

That's obvious enough, yes.

Indeed. You have to be able to judge routine things, or you'll be unable to operate. But let us tell you now that *you need not judge if the purpose of that judgment is to make something right or wrong*. Remember, *observe*.

I need to recognize shenpa and not let it get control: Even if I can never dispel it, I can still recognize it, neutralize it, and reduce its effect on my life.

It is a lifetime's work Simon. Do not underestimate it. But remember a "lifetime" is not what you thought it was, either.

I have many temptations to return to the game, to total immersion, to forget what I want to be and become a player again.

As we said much earlier, once you know what you want to be, the opposite will come into that space. And in that space is your ability to learn and apply yourself. The environment WILL challenge you - for it is there to do so. That is its purpose.

Yes, I know you're right. Shenpas abound!

But don't be despondent. What you are doing is exactly what you want – and if you pause often enough and stay present, you will know it. Everything is exactly as it should be, exactly as you desire it. Truly it is.

I accept that. Yet right now, it seems hard to grasp.

Why?

Because, frankly, I am at a place in life where I am, well, a bit *bored*.

Why does that make it hard to grasp that everything is as it should be and as you desire it? Describe what you mean when you say you are "bored".

Well, I do feel a bit bored, right now. That's all there is to it.

What are you doing?

I am writing this, sitting at a table in the sunshine, next to a swimming pool with a beer at hand… My goodness, listen to me - how can that be boring?

Is it not what you wanted? Is it not the very visualization you set in motion years ago?

Yes. So why do I feel bored or listless, or whatever it is I am feeling? Is it because I have achieved my vision and now I have nothing to work towards? Do I have to come up with a new vision?

Do you desire that?

No - actually, if I am honest, I am feeling lazy – I can't be bothered to do something big and visionary. And that seems wrong!

Perhaps you are not accurately describing your feeling. Do you feel lazy or are you actually content and feeling no need to be doing anything else?

Maybe, but I feel, well, guilty. I feel guilty for not having a plan for creating more, wealth, retirement funds, etc., or attending to the kids. Maybe I'm a bad dad.

Describe what your kids are doing.

They are inside the house. Their friends came over and they are playing with them upstairs.

What are they playing?

Video games on the TV. They love it – they get loud and very involved!

Well, it sounds like you've provided well for them at this moment, Simon...

OK, I get your point, but let me try it this way - I feel I will shortly have to justify myself.

Who to?

Other people, their expectations: Friends, parents, neighbors, etc.

Listen. These other people... They are here helping you with what you desire to be. Whether they antagonize you, bully you, laugh at you or love and shower you with riches, it is all part of what you have chosen, with them, to experience.

So does that mean I should be doing something other than this, or not?

From this moment, what do you want to be?

Not again... OK, I want to be who I am. And I am doing it. I'm Ok with that. But my point is that for some reason that does not always feel comfortable. In fact, sometimes I feel I am living an act... that I'm not really Simon at all, or that what people see is not the real me. Does that make any sense?

How did you think it would feel when you decided you wanted to see the world differently? When the things we have told you and you have remembered in these dialogues began to prove to be the truth?

But – at least I thought it would feel good.

There is no good, remember?

OK but I certainly didn't think it would feel bad!

Does it feel bad? Just pause for a second. Look into your mood and perspective. Does it feel good or bad?

It doesn't feel like anything. I feel kind of tired and spacey. But that's no good. I have to have some "get up and go" to survive around here. And, not feeling that right now, the overall effect is that I feel "bad".

Think about what you experienced over the last few weeks in your corporate work. Have you lacked energy, focus, creativity, drive or passion?

Well, no, I have had a lot, in fact. I have been surprised at my achievements, and my ability (some of the time) to step back away from the game and observe and in doing so stay clear minded and effective.

Indeed, you have achieved more than you used to because of these lessons. Again, don't be hard on yourself. When you need it, you have plenty of drive. Right now you are physically and mentally recovering from the experience of a challenging workload, while also experiencing the world from a different perspective, along with a wholly new view on who and what you are in the universe. Unsurprisingly, it can be quite disorienting.

[Break – I did a short relaxation exercise]

Mmmm. Hold on – that was interesting. For a moment, as I considered what you said but just let it float away, I actually felt a little rush of excitement, dizziness almost, about what I now am. It was very fleeting, though - why is that?

It was fleeting because you tried to grab, hold, analyze and justify it. The little piece of bliss you felt in that moment came when you were not grasping and rationalizing but <u>letting go</u>. You experienced a moment of freedom – of 'nothingness'. That is why some people who meditate describe moments of bliss that they only achieve once - because after that they are seeking too hard to repeat it, trying to catch it again to control and own it. You cannot explain or understand these moments. You can only experience them.

So where does that leave me then? I just carry on? I'm not OK <u>and</u> I'm OK, all at the same time, right?

Take some attention back from your worldly responsibilities. Place trust in yourself and the purpose of your Soul and the gestalt that is the plan of the Oneness. You have to justify yourself to no-one. Return your focus to being what you most desire to be. And then, if an action comes up, take it if you wish. In the meantime, watch your life unfold. It'll happen with or without your self-punishment and guilt.

This is going to be a constant challenge – getting 'disconnected', falling back into the game and then seeking to regain awareness again, right?

You will see.

Review

1. While you have to make routine judgments all the time in your daily life, decline the urge to pass judgments if the purpose is to make something right or wrong – in those cases just observe.

2. Everyone you know and meet is helping you be what you desire to be. Whether your interaction with them feels good or bad to you, it is all part of what you have chosen, with them, to experience.

3. You can achieve moments of bliss by letting go of all the things that keep you bound to this world as a player. And when you achieve those moments, let them happen and *let them be*. If you grab and try to recreate them, they will slip away.

CHAPTER 27

▼

I have a former colleague who is a committed Christian, and each time we meet he restates his position that only one religion can be the right way to God. This is based on his belief that Jesus stated the only way to heaven is through Him… and thus that one right way must be Christianity. He also restated his belief that if we fail to recognize this during our lives, God will send us to hell for eternity.

What is your question?

Why does this trouble me so much?

You tell us.

That's simple - I think it's wrong!

Is it?

Based on all that has gone before in these dialogues and what I have read from other sources, it seems to be.

Are you sure?

No, I am not sure – that's why I am asking!

As we have already told you:

> *All you need to know is what you are not, and that everything is no-thing. Thus, you need to know, nothing...* You continue to seek for right and wrong, but whether something matters (or is matter) is a condition relevant only to the <u>human</u> world. But God *is not* matter and does not *need to* matter. God just is. God is the only truth; He cannot be explained by human logic, although you have needed to come to this point in your journey by using logic. Think of it this way: Logic is just a "path of knowing" on which you can walk and move from one human perspective to another. It is a winding mountain path, up which you walk as you ascend to the highest version of yourself. At the peak is a moment of faith where the path falls away and you step out into *nothing and not knowing.* And there, you find the truth. You cannot know the truth, be given it, buy it, learn it or make it. You cannot describe it or write it. You can only experience and feel it. And only the truth is peace.

OK, again you go over old ground for me. And I think my friend would agree with most of that, except that I think he'd say that the leap of faith requires acceptance of Jesus and that otherwise, it's an eternity of hellfire you're leaping into.

Then that is *his* interpretation, and that of many others. Your interpretation, that God is not jealous, vengeful nor interested in torturing Souls for eternity, is your own. We covered much of this already and need not repeat it here.

OK, but back to my question, which was why does it still bother me when I hear something that contradicts or limits the passage you just repeated?

It bothers you because you don't fully accept or consciously remember all our explanations and our realizations in these dialogues. And you never will.

I never will? What use is it then? What use are any of these dialogues?

Would you like to fully believe what we have discussed and shared with you, without question and with full certainty? Would you like not to have to think about all this anymore?

Maybe...

Then take what you have learned here and declare it your own religion. Accept it with the "leap of faith" required by all religions and go about your business satisfied with the answers you have here. Whether or not you accept what you have learned or subsequently choose a traditional religion, you can live like most of those around you, for whom religious faith is freeing and can end the uncertainty created by true consciousness' constant state of questioning. Would you feel safer that way?

Safer? Perhaps.

Does your friend feel safer, do you think? What did he tell you about the reason for his interest in your viewpoint?

He said that he likes to listen to be sure that he is correct in his commitment to Jesus as his savior.

Do you think he is open to other ideas and possibilities?

He says he is.

At this time he is listening only so as to prove his current beliefs and position.

But hold on - then that is all I am doing! I am no better!

Who said you were better?

Hmmm. Good point.

Here is another perspective of there being no time as you perceive it: Until you actually change your mind, you are not truly open to changing it... Until you are in the moment of changing, you are changeable only in *potential*. You have changed with these dialogues and you have applied them to your life. You will be the same until you change again. Your friend is not open to change until he so desires and then does so.

But supposing he does not want to change – that he is convinced he is right?

That's his decision. Only he knows, in the deepest part of his being, if his spiritual journey and inquiry concludes with a commitment to the religion of Christianity.

OK, but what has this got to do with my question?

Because when you hear things that challenge your thinking, or indicate to you someone has a position from which they cannot or will not move, you sense your own rigidity. Indeed, let us remind you that the rigidity or errors you see in others are only a projection of your own. Remember one of your desired states of being is Open-Minded...

You mean that it's time for me to change again, in some way?

Only when you do.... What we are saying, and said before, is that your environment reflects what you are and where you are in your own evolution. It's not about your friend's lack of willingness, but your own.

I see that now.

Tell us, what has happened today that you have been unable to do for a while, as a result of the discussion with your friend?

I began writing again; I continued work on this book.

Indeed. The experience with your friend was for and about you, not him (although he will also have got something out of the event of course, but that is his business). And thus what you sensed as "troubling" was the arousal of energy for you to move on again, to restart your expansion and spiritual evolution. Now, be willing to interpret old feelings and emotions differently. The old assumptions were to serve you at a different level of consciousness than the one you are now at. A sense of feeling "troubled" is not bad – ask an antelope on the savannah who just escaped a stalking predator.

I understand.

Review

1. The search for spiritual awareness requires an acceptance and state of 'not knowing' all the answers – and thus creates uncertainty. If this state is too uncomfortable, then accept the "leap of faith" into a religion which best matches your beliefs at that time. Stay with it until such a time that your desire to learn more is once again great enough to traverse uncertainty.

2. Until you actually change, you are changeable only in potential. And *potential* is of no value in the current moment.

3. When you sense inflexibility of perspective or ideas in others, you are mirroring your own rigidity. "Listen to all of them, judge none of them."

CHAPTER 28

▼

I am getting an increasing sense that all this analysis and modeling of what is the truth has only been a process by which I could establish a belief in something (indeed *anything*) other than what I used to believe.

You developed your Personal Myth and built upon it. What you had not considered is that the myth itself is one of a myriad of potential models. The creativity in the system is truly limitless. And your creativity, your thinking through what you have here, has created another potentiality and you are choosing it and living it right now.

You mean there is no right answer to the question "what is the universe?"

That would be a fair assumption - and the fact of there being no right or wrong is hardly a new one in these dialogues. But you are seeing things differently now - there is no right or wrong at ANY level. As Allan Watts suggested, by the act of establishing the *possibility* of something, it is already done. Every thought you have, every explanation you come up with, for anything, is a creation – and one in which you can participate if you know how to claim it[13]. This is what is meant where you have seen warnings to not underestimate your creative power.

---

13 You can "claim" the alternative experience by "feeling the feeling as though it has already come true" (Gregg Braden, Speaking The Lost Language of God, Audio CD, 2005).

Everything is chaos then... There is no definitive explanation for *anything*?

There is an explanation for everything - *just many of them*. Right and wrong is a concept relevant only in your world. Do you understand that this is another way to see what we described about there being no good or bad? There just is, and the 'is' exists in every way that can be imagined by God. And that is infinite, a world without end?

Wait a minute then. So is this how we really have creative power? Anything we think, big or small has the true potentiality to happen. And at some level, I, as part of God, choose which ones to play out, and how. And the scale of that happening, big or small, as *A Course in Miracles* puts it, does not matter since all of them are the same to God.

That is a way to look at it.

And my need to understand this, to see a pattern and logic to it, is about my need to control it. So, the choice I make now (if I can take a leap of faith) is whether to let go of trying to understand and control things, and just go with it.

OK.

But what would I be 'going with', exactly?

You can go with what you create or what others create. Or you can choose to fight it – which is what most people do, most of the time.

So, this dialogue has led me to a point where I have created an explanation of what the truth is, but that's only one possibility. The only thing that's fixed is that the world is not what I thought it was... But that's not true either is it? The world as I thought it

was is only a possibility. In fact, it's one I am within, in a very real way. Boy... This is like a spiral and I'm getting dizzy.

Go on.

Because of the limitless flexibility of all this, an advanced being could create not only events in a human life, but the very infrastructure of all that is, the very fabric of the universe. Everything just is and exists in every way that God can imagine, all at once, through me.

Are you frustrated by the thought that there is no fixed answer?

Yes and no. I feel that I should be annoyed that all along, there has been no right answer. And that you've been kind of playing with me.

If we had told you this from the start, would you have come this far? Would you be able to have any faith in your conclusion to this point in any way whatsoever?

No, probably not.

Then you understand what happened here, then.

I'm not sure where that leaves me... But then again, maybe I am. I no longer have to seek the *right* answer - it is any and all of them. Hey - *that turns the meaning of life from the need to be right to the need to be creative*!

A beautiful thought is it not?

That's what made the great inventors keep on trying, I guess. I can choose and create without being concerned about being right or wrong. As you have kept on telling me, I cannot fail. Before, I thought that meant eventually I will get the right answer, win the game, but it really means that I cannot fail because there is

nothing to get right. Or wrong. There just is. That's pretty cool, actually. What now?

Keep these insights with you as much as you can each day. Seek for moments of amazement and peace in not needing to know or understand everything. Just be, and seek to understand now what is meant by listening to the space in-between. For what you considered nothing is not nothing, but all that is true.

Review

1. Everything we think creates a potentiality, the scale of which, big or small, does not matter because all of them are the same to God.

2. We can claim each potentiality we create - That is why our thoughts are powerful.

3. Our need to understand the purpose of this world, to see cause and effect and logic to it, is created by our desire to control it in physical terms. Spiritual liberation and access to our true creative powers requires us to let go of that desire and *go with our own flow*. This is part of knowing and following what you want to be.

4. If you can release the need to be right, you can turn the meaning of your life from the need to win to the freedom to be creative.

CHAPTER 29

▼

I would like to ask about a meditation exercise that I have been using successfully for a while – but which spontaneously changed for me recently.

Why?

Because I think that the change represents a fundamental shift in my perspective.

Let's start with the original image.

OK. For several months I have pictured this image each morning as I prepared for work. In it, I see some distance from me, a crystal – a specific one which I purchased in New Mexico at Christmas 2006, and keep in my office. In the image, the space between the crystal and me forms a kind of clear tube, like a glass tunnel under the sea. And in the "sea" outside the tunnel, are the ongoing events of the day as I focus and move toward the crystal. I found this image to be a helpful way of conceptualizing my path through the turmoil and challenges of day to day life.

Why did that help?

Because it assisted me in seeing that the world will go on

and that it need not be something which distracts me. Most importantly, the tube provides me a window from which I can observe the world quite separately from myself.

Now tell us about the change that has happened in the image.

Well, quite without intending it, one morning the tunnel turned inside out! Instead of the tunnel (me) being on the inside of the activity of the world, the tunnel went through *my* experience – indeed seemingly through *me*. So, the world was a part of me instead of me being a part of the world!

What else?

Well, the wall of the tunnel was not glass through which I looked but a membrane which *interacts* with the world inside the tunnel – i.e. it *feels*, biologically, this human experience.

Go on.

So, far from inanimate, the tunnel is alive and part of the humanness of me. So now my image is of what I can best describe as a bubble through which I know the tunnel runs – but I am the bubble, not the tunnel (or something inside the tunnel).

Your original image with the crystal served its purpose in showing you how to separate yourself from day to day matters and focus on your purpose. Now you have glimpsed another level that has enabled you to see that you are not within or trapped by worldly activities. On the contrary, those activities are within you while you experience them as part of yourself.

But, somehow I think there's a lot more I am not seeing – can you help me?

We will use your "bubble" symbol:

1. The process of turning the original image inside out is not a single event. You need to realize that both states and perspectives are *current*.
2. You can go forward <u>and backwards</u> in the tunnel – on the outside of the tunnel, each scene of the movie of your life experience is playing simultaneously and you can watch it from any point in the tunnel. Each time you watch it, it may change based on your perspective and desires – present AND past. Remember, however, that there is no actual timeline here - it's all concurrent.
3. The inside-out 'flip' you describe continues outwards (and inwards for that matter) in that the bubble is also part of another tunnel - which itself runs through a larger bubble, and so forth. And this multiplication is without limit.
4. There can be more than one tunnel in one bubble and each one represents a potentiality of experience such as those we have discussed.
5. The tunnels are not in parallel; they intersect, cross and merge as, indeed, do the contents of other bubbles.
6. Your concept of the tunnel in the bubble is an analogy for your relationship with your soul.

Boy – that's a lot to get my head around.

We seek to provide you with a new perspective with which you can change not only your view of the world but, and more importantly, the core <u>beliefs</u> with which you consciously and subconsciously create your experiences and the world you perceive.

Review

1. You can view your life as a tunnel that runs through the external world, along which you proceed. This image can help you advance toward your desired goal and minimize external distractions of your day to day life.

2. Or, you can consider yourself as a greater whole – a bubble through which your current life, your alternative lives, and even those of others, pass. With this perspective, you can see that you are not trapped within externally independent world activities: Your life occurs *within yourself.*

3. If you can also imagine that the lives of others travel through the bubble, then you can understand that they truly are part of *you.*

4. If you can grasp this bubble concept, you are beginning to understand yourself as a Soul and therefore closer to bridging back to your source.

CHAPTER 30

▼

I am trying to apply what I have learned, and interested in understanding more about how someone (including me) really changes; how people can move to a place of demonstrating a heightened level of consciousness or enlightenment, as it were, in their day-to-day life. Obviously I don't mean disappearing up to heaven or anything like that... I am thinking more about how one begins to actually live and apply spiritual lessons as they are learned. In my case, for example, how I fully live what I have written in this book.

What's the difference today, compared to your interest in this in our previous discussions?

Well, I thought that at some point I would have learned enough to change and be very different – something would, well, 'click' and happen to me.

You change in small steps as you accumulate your human life experiences. For example, the way your appearance changes, along with deeper elements such as your values, beliefs and motivations. You *have* changed as a result of this work, you know!

Yes, but I am talking about a specific moment at which I am aware that I have significantly changed - not just internally but

in my behaviors. I'm talking about, as they say "revolution not evolution".

First of all, remember what we told you: "Until you are in the moment of changing, you are changeable only in *potential*... You will be the same until you change again."
Second, a question: Why do you seek to accelerate your progress?

Because I would like to see some more results! The way I think and see the world *has* changed, like you say, but I am feeling that if I can't see a big difference, what's the point?

What is your real question here? Are you asking how you can change, or whether you <u>should</u> in order to prove your progress?

OK - perhaps my question is really this: Does it <u>matter</u> if I change externally, in the physical world? Is it necessary?

It matters if it matters to <u>you,</u> and if it matters to you, it matters to your perception of <u>everyone else</u>.

It matters to me because I want to be a higher version of myself, as we said in previous dialogues. And that includes making positive changes in my present human life.

OK, then.

So it matters to me. I already knew that!

But did you understand our point that *because* it matters to you, it matters (i.e. influences) your perception of <u>everyone else</u>.

Not really – but now you make a point of it, it means because of something I believe about myself, I perceive (and judge) my whole experience with that expectation in mind.

Indeed, you <u>expect</u> other people to have the same intention to change – to constantly live their true beliefs or at least those which they claim are their beliefs. How well is that belief serving you?

Not too well, I guess. But let's step back here - I can accept that it's fruitless for me to expect people to behave in line with their stated beliefs...

Don't get confused between what you think their beliefs are and what they actually are – you don't know the true beliefs of most people you know and therefore cannot judge if they behaving in line with them or not.

OK, and fair point, but do they, at some level desire to behave better - so as to be more in line with their spiritual development?

Behave better in whose opinion? Yours?

Please answer the question - Do other people want to change in line with their spiritual development?

Again, it's about <u>you</u>. You seem to think others should change. For example, look how frustrated you get when you see folks attending religious events and organizations who do not seem to change the way they live their lives. "Hypocrites!" you cry.

Yes, that's true. So what are you saying?

If changing your human behaviors and physical experiences is how you want to measure your steps to the next highest version of yourself, then it matters a great deal to you. But listen - *What causes you discomfort is that you assume that others must or should think the same way... when, clearly, not all of them do.* Either in terms of their willingness to change or what they want to change to or from!

But why would they not? Shouldn't they <u>want</u> to change?

Not necessarily - they have a different purpose for their lives. Remember, you are observing them. They either don't even consider they need to change anything externally (except perhaps attending church or performing rituals), or have chosen to fulfill their growth internally, with no external (visible) change at all. Consider also that, because of where you live, your direct observations are largely of Christians, and many of them consider that whatever they have done, they will go to heaven based on a timely declaration of their faith, not their worldly behavior. Indeed, other religions require an act you would call barbaric in order to achieve God's blessing.

Agh, I know – I am judging them...

Remember, there is no good or bad. Such values exist only in your interpretation of your own experiences. An action is only what is done - whether it is good or bad is based on a subjective evaluation after the event, and can change based on the observer's perspective and scope of consideration, and even subsequent related events over time (or at least what you perceive as time). We will talk about this more later.

OK, I understand that.

So, back to your question about others changing (or not) - Is judging others' behaviors in this regard helping you?

I don't know. How would I know if it's helping?

How does it feel when you do it?

Do you mean does it feel good? I feel *superior,* if that's what you mean (which is not a good thing, I know).

Drop the good and bad and judgmental thoughts. Instead, think in terms of whether you feel comfort or discomfort.

Like I said, I feel superior. But now you come to mention it, the

overall sensation is of anger and frustration – so that's *discomfort* then. That far outweighs the sense of superiority, which, actually, is not one of comfort either... Why do I feel like that?

Try Byron Katie's approach – what she calls The Work: First, state what annoys you.

OK, here goes: "It really aggravates me to see people who claim to be spiritual or religious believers behave badly. It makes me think they are hypocrites and even liars and I strongly dislike them for that."

Is all that true?

It certainly <u>looks</u> that way. And it's true that I dislike them for it.

Can you be sure? Can you be sure that every time you make that judgment that a) The person you are observing is a committed spiritual or religious person; b) Their actions are deliberately and flagrantly in violation of their beliefs; c) that you really dislike these people, most of whom you have not even properly met, let alone know?

Well, no. I am making a lot of assumptions.

You have already said how it makes you feel and react when make assumptions – superior, angry and frustrated. None of those are likely to be feelings that you want to sustain, and we suggest you consider ending the habit. So next, "turn it around" as Byron Katie says.

OK... It really aggravates me when <u>I</u> claim to be spiritual... but behave badly.

And again...

It really aggravates <u>other people</u> when <u>I</u> claim to be spiritual, and then behave badly.

Go on.

It makes me think I am a hypocrite and a liar and I strongly dislike myself for that. And, I guess, it makes others think I am a hypocrite and a liar... ...I get the point.

Indeed. *Your frustration with those people is a projection of your frustration with your own perceived lack of progress.*

Ouch – but a good ouch. I can go with that. But – they, other people, are still behaving wrongly, hypocritically, aren't they?

What they are doing does not matter.

Hold on: Even if I were to be doing everything I think I should (note I did not say "right"), they would <u>still</u> be behaving hypocritically, wouldn't they?

It's how you perceive the world that matters. Remember that you can't change the world through judgment. Instead, as we have told you, you must transcend it through impartial observation, depthless love, and unending forgiveness. As you achieve such a perspective, you will, naturally, cease to judge what others are doing and see that it matters not what they do. As the story of Jesus describes, of those men who killed him he said "Forgive them Father, for they know not what they do".

All right, but where does that leave me with my initial question: Does it matter if I change externally, in the physical world? Is it something I should be doing?

First, and this is absolutely key for you, our guidance is that once you begin to truly accept what you desire to be, your 'external' <u>will</u>

change... because you will act on your desires and your external experience and persona will change without direct effort.

Second, stop looking for approval and for what you should be doing to appease or impress other people (or God for that matter). Again, this matters because it matters to you. At this point, this issue is being clouded and blocked by your annoyance with others because you project your own sense of failure to change from yourself onto them. Your sense of superiority, and assumption that if others don't need to change then neither do you, makes this even more difficult for you.

Wait! I never said that if others don't need to change then neither do I!

But is that in the back of your mind? Is that not a strong underlying excuse for you not to make the changes you really want to make?

Agh... Yes, I suppose it is.

Alright, then.

Help me move past this problem then... please.

Here are some suggestions:

1. If you now know that your frustration with others is really frustration with yourself, you can defuse this when it starts to arise.
2. Step forward with a belief that you can change; become that higher version of yourself and *there is no need to wait for others to do the same.*
3. As we have said, if you truly accept what you desire to be, your 'external' world will change.
4. To change yourself you must change your *perspective*. Remember something you yourself said in a talk you gave to a business forum at Texas Christian University (TCU) in

2007: "If you move your body but leave your perspective unchanged, then you remain unmoved."

Review

1. Self-discovered spiritual change usually comes in small steps as you accumulate your human life experiences.

2. If something matters deeply to you then it greatly influences your perception of others, including creating an expectation that they feel (or should feel) the same way. In reality, they have their own (and completely valid) agendas about which you have no knowledge (but many assumptions).

3. Once you <u>truly</u> know what you desire to be, you will change... because you will act on your desires and your external experience (and persona) will change without pretence.

4. "If you move your body but leave your perspective unchanged, then you remain unmoved."

CHAPTER 31

▼

Following on from the previous chapter and watching the development of others, does a person's underlying 'character' drive their level or awareness or vice versa?

Expand on your question.

OK. A person's character seems to be highly reflective of his or her inner strength and condition. I wonder if a strong character is someone who seems that way because they have a level of enlightenment, or if they achieved a level of enlightenment because they have a strong character. Kind of the 'chicken and egg' thing...

The character you observe in someone is just what they are at that moment – to YOU: Your judgment of their strength and rightness of character is purely subjective and based on your own perspective at that moment. It's totally relative to you and can change in an instant with something as simple as a cuss or a kiss.

OK – regardless of perceived quality of character, then, what is it that makes a person the character they are?

In the term itself lies some of the answer. As we have said before, Shakespeare's words were quite correct when he wrote "all the world's a stage and all the men and women merely players". Your character is the one through which you interact with your chosen life experience.

But who defines my character?

You do.

My Soul or me, the man?

Both (since they are really the same), but then you, the man, develop it in human experience. Your character here as a man is the vessel in which you travel through life and respond to the world.

But what about evil people, or "bad" characters? Do they choose to be bad, or are they born that way?

They are born that way, become that way and are that way, through choice. Remember there is no good or bad on the larger scale of things when you accept that everything is relative. These 'bad characters' as you call them are genuinely being their version of "right" or "good".

Come now – did Hitler (about as bad a man as I can think of) really believe he was *good*?

He believed that his actions were correct because they made him feel what he felt as "good"... And feelings are a large part of what the worldly experience is about. Listen, this is an over simplification, but the *feeling* of any one person's 'good' is the same, but the impact of its root cause is different depending on whether it's coming from a position of fear or love.

But if you are saying that Hitler was coming from fear, then isn't there a level of judgment there? Specifically, if he was *afraid* it was only because deep down he feared retribution for his bad actions?

He feared loss of control and power - and failure. As do many people with what you might call 'good intentions'. Listen – this is very important: *Love is not a state of being good but one of being unafraid.*

But I could be a fearless <u>monster</u>!

Indeed you could. Do you want to be?

No.

Well, that's your choice then. Are you still seeking ways to prove things right and wrong, and the judgment thereof?

No, not intentionally – but maybe I am. But anyway, what's all that got to do with my question about Character?

"Character" is a loaded word. There is an assumption that strength of character means that a person is "good". Character has been defined as having conviction of what is right and a sense of guilt for past bad actions (i.e. a sense of right and wrong). In fact, character, as such, is not important.

What?

Anyone's character is just a shell via which they perform their role in the game and is in the domain of the play. As an Observer you can step OUT of character. In fact, your ability to observe DEPENDS on your ability to step out of your character.

So what are you saying?

That you should avoid defining yourself or others via observed strength of character. Consider:
  a) Human 'character' is a disguise through which to observe others
  b) You should develop your own character to suit your

purpose in becoming what you want to be... in the knowledge that neither your character nor its qualities are the end goal.

Wait... If other people already do that, then people who I think are bad characters and Players may be 'conscious' after all... they may be <u>Observers</u> after all. There may be more Observers than I thought!

Would that make a difference to how you observe <u>them</u>?

Yes. And it's another way to realize that this world is not what it seems. But frankly, I really don't think I am encountering very many Observers - I struggle to believe that some of the less savory characters I encounter are Observers still playing a role (via their character).

Why do you think that?

Because most people seem to be, well, caught up in participating fully in what is largely a tough world and bad behavior.

You mean you consider them too "bad" to be Observers?

Yes, because I have assumed that once you're an Observer you will be behaving well!

As we said in an earlier chapter, Observers know that good and evil are necessary opposites. They are being the next highest version of themselves in the knowledge of their chosen purpose of your world. Now, think about yourself for a moment. Do you consider yourself an Observer?

Some of the time, I hope!

OK - Do you think everyone looks at you and sees you behave well

(i.e. how <u>they</u> think you should behave) all or even most of the time?
Well, no, probably not.

Indeed – because it's totally subjective and relative. Even if you genuinely believe you behave well (or do the right thing) all of the time, someone else will (genuinely) not see it that way. To win, there has to be a loser. Indeed, a 'character' is a highly unstable entity since it is viewed differently by each person.

Yes - As a good friend of mine said, "you have a million reputations based on your *perceived* character." I guess I can't win, right?

Now, if you accept that good and evil are necessary opposites, and that often you "can't win" as you just put it, tell me why you resist the thought that Observers may be playing their role in ways you find less than acceptable?

I resist because I had an assumption that the effect of the 'consciousness' that an Observer has is the same across all people – and that effect was to seek to be better, nicer, and kinder to others.

We explained this earlier but let's go over it again here. You already know that good is not better than bad. Both are valid. And you just concluded that you "can't win" because someone will interpret your behavior as negative even if you intended otherwise. So listen – *The state of true Observing is <u>neutral</u> and has nothing to do with the action of the Observer*. Think of it this way: Consider a small child – she may pull the legs off a bug <u>but just to see what happens</u> and with no 'malice aforethought'.

Good point – and I guess that powerful people may have known what you have taught me (and perhaps been what we here call Observers) for hundreds of years, but used it to maintain power, wealth and control... or at least for, shall we say, 'less than selfless purposes'.

What does that make you think?

I guess increasing human consciousness does not necessarily mean a move towards the nice, enlightened world I like to imagine and dream about... and explains why so little progress <u>seems</u> to be being made toward it.

Go on.

All this is about me letting go of judging right and wrong and remembering I cannot change the world but need to see (and participate in it) differently. Just like you have told me, all along, right?

One step at a time.

OK but hold on. This is very disappointing. I had hoped that there are a growing number of people who want to make the world a better place. But you keep telling me this life is not about making the world a better place, right?

First, people could make the world a better place if they wanted to, but that's not its <u>purpose</u>: It's not the objective end result, despite what many people believe. Second, and as we have told you many times, your life here has nothing to do with doing good or bad. It has nothing to do with <u>judging</u> others, or yourself, against the polarities of right and wrong. Your life is for you to experience what your Soul set out to experience. Being an Observer does not mean being better than a Player, it's just a level of awareness which increases your freedom of choice; a 'truth that will set you free'.

Review

1. Your character is the vessel through which you interact with your chosen life experience. Whether that character is perceived as strong or otherwise is highly subjective and likely to change based on events and shifting of beliefs over time.

2. Even if you genuinely believe you behave well (or do the right thing) all of the time, not everyone will see it that way.

3. People could make the world a better place if they wanted to, but that is not its purpose.

CHAPTER 32

▼

This is a most disagreeable world, isn't it? Every time I turn on the news on the TV or read a newspaper, there's so much trouble, strife, and bad news.

So those stories and events are disagreeable to you. Why?

Because people are doing things that I'd like them not to, or not doing things I would like them to do.

So you disagree with what's going on?

Yes. That's my point.

In that case, it's not that the world is disagreeable, but you.

Isn't that just semantics?

No. Think about it - Do the people you see on the news have the choice to agree with you?

Come on - I'm just a little guy out there and they don't even know I exist. But they have the choice to do what I think is a better thing because it's usually a pretty obvious option and is shared by many others.

But do they have the chance to agree with <u>you</u>?

I'm just not in a position to tell them!

Yes you are.

Maybe some of them, but not, say the President of the USA. I can't tell him anything!

Yes you can. There is always something you can do to get a message across.

What, like jumping over the wall at the Whitehouse and getting shot?

A drastic measure for sure, but you'd get noticed.

This is not about me getting noticed.

Is it not?

No, it's about my frustration at not liking much of what I see. And that it makes me think there's no point in changing myself.

We talked about this already so we won't go over it again here. But perhaps it is more about your need to be noticed than you think...

That makes me sound like an egotistical person. I don't think I am.

Don't get defensive – it stops you from listening. There is nothing wrong with desiring to be noticed (or anything else for that matter). It's a problem only if you deny it or are unable to identify with your unconscious intention.

My "unconscious intention"... What would that be?

Do you want people to have the insights that you have at this time and in doing so, perhaps change their ways?

Yes. What's wrong with that?

Nothing - unless you make it into an assumption that others are either too stupid to understand you, too evil to agree, or just plain wrong. Isn't that what's really underneath your discomfort at watching what's going on in the world?

Hey, this seems to be turning into a case of "it's _my_ problem". Feels like a guilt trip...

Any problem is always your problem. You choose to make it that way, or not, in the judgment you make of the people and circumstances. The rest of the world goes on, either way.

So what are you saying? That I should just let it go?

That's what we have been telling you.

Yes, that's true. But at some point, don't I have to think about changing these external things before they begin to influence me personally?

Are they influencing you very much, personally?

They are starting to. And they will probably have a huge impact on me.

When?

I don't know - in the not too distant future I guess.

Remember there is only now. And you choose the now and your reaction to it in the very instant of experience. If you do not want to experience something, then you won't.

But I have experienced bad things.

When?

In the past...

From fear of the future to fear of the past... Again - there is no past, only now. Your past is relevant only as the experiences you remember and resulting *beliefs* you gained that now influence your responses to current experiences - and form your future. Look around you, right now... and anyone reading this, please do the same. What is happening?

It's quiet, and peaceful, and I am writing this – but that's not the point! Look, for example, the global economy is going down the tubes.

Right now, is your economic status OK?

Yes, I suppose it is. But that could change tomorrow or sometime in the future.

We cannot emphasize enough the need for you to release the concept of time, as we told you before. As we just said, there is only now and your ability to accept that fully will remove much of your distress in this matter. Don't miss out on what you have today for the fear of losing it tomorrow.

OK.

But now, we also need to explain to you that the world outside your immediate awareness is not relevant in the way you think it is. Nothing exists with direct meaning to you unless you are observing it, now. In quantum mechanics terms, unless you are observing it, then the wave functions of the world beyond your observation have many possible states.

So what does that mean?

It means that <u>you define and create your future in the current moment</u>. That definition of the future is driven to a greater or lesser extent by the amount of power you give to the collective consciousness. Those who are not conscious, the "Players" as we have called them, are totally at the mercy of the collective and their own unconscious beliefs and assumptions which they contribute to the collective consciousness. You, on the other hand, and others who are more aware, have a far greater level of control over your immediate experiences, and future. The amount of your influence on your experiences and future, and its very nature, are driven by the beliefs you hold dearest.

Please explain that...

For example, people with strong structured religious beliefs will experience events influenced heavily by the tenets and doctrines of their religion. On the other hand, your experience is and will be based more on your own beliefs (such as those you detail in these writings). Your recent changes in this regard are creating quite different experiences (and possible future potentialities) are they not?

Yes.

It's essential to know that these changes are occurring because your beliefs have changed at a deep level. Superficial or pretended changes in beliefs do not work that way and that is why many people who try new religions or the "create your own reality" approaches without true changes to their core belief systems are disappointed with the results.

So, let me get this straight. My current experiences and future are defined less by what I see reported and predicted on the news, and more by what I believe at the deepest level. It's <u>my</u> *beliefs* that create <u>my</u> world, while the world at large develops anyway based on collective consciousness. And, I guess, some of those beliefs are buried in my subconscious - finding them and working on them would be hugely beneficial.

Does that make sense to you?

Yes, actually it does. It's why people who have a truly positive nature and outlook have what seem to be happier lives, I guess. But where does that leave me with my original question: Why would I bother to seek a higher version of myself when I still see most of what's going on in the world as hopeless and disagreeable?

The fact that you see an external world (beyond your immediate experience) which looks less than attractive to you does not have a direct correlation with your own life experience, which is driven by you, in this instant. <u>Your</u> increased level of awareness at this moment provides the ability to react to and choose your experience to a much greater extent than those people who are embroiled in the "game" of the collective consciousness. Tying this back to a previous Chapter, you don't have to try to change yourself or the world – you just have to know your beliefs and choose what you want to be, and from there the actions and experiences will follow. And thusly will you contribute to the world in the role which was your true calling. As we have said and as is explained in *A Course in Miracles*, you can choose to see the world differently. And even if you cannot change the world overnight, you can exist within it with peace and hope and the experiences you desire.

Review

1. Whether or not something is a problem is your choice – based on how you judge the people and circumstances. Either way, the reality continues, all the same, regardless of your judgment.

2. Your past provides the experiences that create your <u>beliefs</u> - which not only influence your responses to current experiences, but also form your future.

3. Identifying and working on your <u>beliefs</u> (which are at the root of your emotional triggers), especially those that are buried deep in your subconscious, are very beneficial activities in spiritual growth and handling life's challenges.

CHAPTER 33

▼

I recently saw a scene from a TV show where a lawyer is passionately describing all the positive things that could have been done with the money spent on the war in Iraq.

OK. What do you want to discuss about it?

The point is not the war, at all, is it? The real point is that 'the system' does not want to do the alternatives the character lists - healthcare, fuel conservation, and education. Paying for those things (and ending the war) would put the whole system out of whack and shift the balance of power. And that's the true no-no, isn't it?

You are right in that the point is not the war - indeed stopping the war will change nothing. You could provide healthcare, fuel conservation, education, whatever, <u>and</u> have a war, if you really desired to. The resources are all there, limited only by the same sense of lack and apathy that we previously defined as the reason for people's need for religion... but whereas religious systems relieve the need to take responsibility for the development of a personal path to spirituality, monetary systems relieve the need to take responsibility for the development of your worldly experience - and true potential. Both religious and monetary systems are based on the use of a 'currency' of which there is limited supply. Most importantly, these currencies are the very entities of which lack or plenty provide <u>definitions and measure</u> of strength or weakness, happiness or sadness or even good and evil.

That makes sense, but isn't the real issue the greedy and power-hungry people running these systems?

Your ego is projecting guilt onto others instead of facing up to what you need to change about yourself - <u>your</u> role in the systems that you are so keen to blame for the problems of the world.

Explain, please.

What is important for you to see here is that this is not about a group of mean-minded leaders, Capitalism, or whatever you see as "The System". Rather, it is about the truth that <u>you</u> cannot see past the religious and monetary systems which you have bought-into, and that create the very lack about which you are so angry (and afraid).

Ouch. How do I break out of my current beliefs and perceptions then? I can't change all this!

Indeed. All along we have told you that you cannot change the world. But, let us put it this way: Rebels declare their liberation <u>before</u> they trigger their physical rebellion - which is simply attacking, dismantling and dispensing with the systems of religion, commerce or government with which they disagree.

But if that has happened in the past, haven't such rebels just slipped back into the old ways and rebuilt the old stuff all over again, but by another name? And if so, why?

Because in your chosen potentiality, most of the rebels' new solutions have been limited to worldly and practical *systems*, so even if they replaced the old ways with something better, they were still inherently flawed.

So I guess that means that the enlightenment of the rebels was wasted... Perhaps when they died, those that came after them were not enlightened in the same way... Have we consistently failed to pass on our lessons to our children? Is the <u>education</u> system the root issue here?

You are back to creating new 'systems', just as all the 'rebels' before you.

Am I a rebel? That's not a label that I feel good about.

Are you not resisting control and tradition?

Yes, but rebels are usually considered traitors to the government and leadership, right? Today, people who are questioning the war in Iraq, for example, are called "unpatriotic" and disapproved of by many people.

It's all perspective and sequencing. George Washington was a rebel to the British system... Until he won, and then he became a hero. And then he defined, and became the new 'system'. By the time these words are read by others, changes will have occurred regarding your war in Iraq, and its causes.

OK. Point made. But what about my idea that education is the root issue?

Your theory that freedom is lost as the original rebels die because they don't teach their children what they learned is an interesting one... So let me ask you this - Do you think anyone could have taught <u>you</u> what you now believe as a result of these dialogues?

No, probably not. I had to find out for myself in my own time, in many ways and from many sources.

But think on this - Even if education is the problem, what difference does that conclusion actually make?

We need to change the education system!

Stop looking at this and other matters from a human historical and anthropological perspective. This is about <u>you</u> and your personal spiritual liberation BEYOND this worldly experience, in this lifetime. As we have said, your task here is not to change the world - this is all about changing yourself; liberating yourself; choosing to see the world differently.

That's hard to swallow: It seems pointless to be an observing non-participant.

You have been forever changed. You cannot go back and participate in the world as a pure Player even if you want to. You have already stepped from the edge of the path of life - now it's a matter of where you want to go, where you desire to land. The level of enlightenment you achieve in this human life does not matter. You have broken free, and <u>that</u> is your victory. Your friend RC says we "cannot escape" this life – but you <u>have</u> escaped. It's just frustrating for you to know that you cannot change the world - just as rebels cannot create lasting, idealistic, post-revolutionary societies.

So that makes me realize something - *Freedom comes before action, not after it.*

Review

1. Our world has everything we need in it to live fulfilled lives. However, our use of currency systems - not just financial (trading money) but other things like religions (trading salvation and forgiveness) education (trading information and prestige) – <u>creates the need for lack</u> - in order to create profitable demand for the currencies.

2. The lack or plenty of these currencies directly define societal statuses and attitudes – not just wealth or poverty but strength or weakness, happiness or sadness, better or worse, and even right and wrong. These statuses and attitudes obscure the abundance we have around us.

3. Freedom comes before action, not after it. Rebels don't fight to win freedom but to *keep* it once they *declare themselves* (which is all it takes): The same can be said for those seeking spiritual freedom – and that's you!

CHAPTER 34

––––––––––▼––––––––––

If there is no such thing as time, why do spiritual teachers use or refer to it?

Because time is fundamental to the way their students think; it is an essential construct of the human experience.

But you have said that everything has already happened, and newly created potentialities also occur instantaneously (even if they play out locally in terms of apparently real time for participants). So how can that be true and the yet teachers still talk about the future?

Future potentialities have happened - but not 'yet' in <u>your</u> current human perspective.

Help me understand that!

Because the passing of time and sequential events are an anchor of your human experience, you naturally think that if we say "everything has already occurred", it did so (at some level) in a linear, time-influenced way. But it didn't. Your default to think in terms of time and sequence prevents you from fully conceiving what we tell you about this.

I see – so tell me again, then.

What happens beyond your dimension, at a high macro level, occurs without time and does not require sequential actions. Think in terms of the *thought* of building a wall compared to actually building it. Thought is not bound by sequence.

That makes sense - Go on.

All of your time-bound experiences are a small part of a larger, non-time bound reality. Time is only part of <u>your</u> experience in your dimension; it's not relevant in the bigger scheme of things. Think of it this way: If you look at a photograph taken from space of a city on Earth, millions of individual events were occurring at the street level when the picture was taken, but you cannot see them in the image. But more importantly, they are not <u>relevant</u> in what you observe because the image exists as a complete and valid entity.

What's your point here?

That you should try not to think in terms of what has happened or will be. You must think in terms of what you know to be the larger truth, which, when known by those who are becoming more aware, means they can see *through* time. Think of looking at a roll of coins, where each coin represents a time-bound event. Looking at the roll from the side, there are many coins, one after the other. But if you look at one end, square-on, you see only one coin, but you *know* the others are there and that the content and the weight of the collective object is the same. We are suggesting you look at the end coin only - in the trust and understanding that there are other coins behind it, and without which it would not be *where* or even *what* it is.

I'm confused.

Logic requires a linear set of evaluations and cause and effect relationships. This is not required when you look at everything as a completed whole at which time you can see that effects are not only the results of causes, but are also the ever-growing roots of their own originating causes. This is another way to think of the "mesh of potentialities" we told you about. From a God-like perspective, you don't have to live with the consequences of an action because that action was taken in full and immediate knowledge of all its originating potentialities (including motive) <u>and</u> all of its effects.

I am still struggling here.

You consider that human life is about living with the results of your actions and deeds: And from a human 'player' perspective that's true. But as we have said many times, the apparent realness of your life is only required for the potentiality to be valid (at some level at least). In and of itself, <u>the potentiality experience is not the point</u>

Whoa - Isn't this world all about the potentiality experience? Isn't the very purpose of my world to provide the environment in which human experiences can, literally be "felt"?

That is one of its purposes. But our message is that the <u>experience</u> is not the point.

This is a big next step, right? OK, so what is the point?

The point is <u>the idea or the creation</u> of the potentiality experience. Now, most of these ideas are beyond your human comprehension. But for those of you who awaken to a higher level of consciousness, you begin to see that the ideas and potentialities expand and converge to create wholly new creations (including new *consciousnesses*) far beyond the experiences you see with your human eyes. As a human, you can only catch a glimpse of simple versions of such things in physical terms - in the form of groundbreaking creative efforts (e.g. art or inventions), feelings (e.g. intuitions or prophesies) or events (e.g. coincidences or amazing feats).

Oh boy. So what does this mean to me?

You can engage in life in a new way because you can choose to know that the point of it is _non-linear creativity, not linear activity_. Knowing this enables true 'Observing' and greater freedom of will.

Can you explain that more fully?

Much of your difficulty in Observing is that you are compelled to get involved like a Player because you feel responsible for parts of the events and processes you see before you. If you can release that compulsion, Observing becomes easier. As we said above, "*From a God-like perspective, you don't have to live with the consequences of an action because that action was taken in full and immediate knowledge of all its originating potentialities... and all of its effects.*" God's creativity is free and spontaneous because it is not limited to precursory actions or conditions, and neither is it limited to or by the results it creates. *And, as part of God, what you will and create is no less valid than the creativity of God itself.*

That sounds a bit arrogant to me...

To deny it would be like saying the fingers of the artist don't produce the painting.

Whew, this is a lot to take in. What's the bottom line here?

This is another lesson in 'seeing the world differently'. While you cannot see the entire gestalt of God, you now have a better idea of what it is – a self-generating and ever-expanding mass of creativity and possibilities... but more importantly, you know that your world is not the end game; it's just one place where possibilities are experienced.

That makes me think about the wave function collapse in Quantum Mechanics... Reality as I see it exists because I observe it – until I observe a wave as a particle, possibilities are limitless. What you are saying is very similar – that my world is just one place where possibilities are experienced and within that, my personal world

is just one set of those possibilities made real. But where does that leave me with time?

Time as you think of it exists only as a construct of your world and perceptions. It is as changeable as any other element of which you can think. As we said above, you can engage in life in a new way because you now know that the point of life is *non-linear creativity*, not *linear (time bound) activity*.

Review

1. God's creation is instantaneous; it occurs without time and does not involve sequential actions. Think in terms of the *thought* of building something, compared to the *act* of building it. Thought forms (which I consider closer to God's nature than our physical world) are neither time nor sequence bound.

2. Our purpose in this world is not just the experience itself - but the embodiment of the idea or creation from and for which the experience was created. We enable our Soul (and therefore God) to expand and create anew - far beyond what we experience in our current potentiality.

3. The point of life is non-linear creativity, not linear (time and consequence bound) activity. Sound complicated? Let me put it in more familiar words: Live in the moment, and less in the fear of the future! As the saying goes: "Remember yesterday, dream about tomorrow, but live for today." Believing this will help you be an Observer.

CHAPTER 35

▼

Are good and evil real and underlying truths – if only because most people agree and have a subconscious sense of what they are?

Are you suggesting that good and evil exist because an individual can define and/or a majority of a collective society can agree on what behaviors are associated with each?

No. What I am trying to get at is that good and evil are underlying truths because I can do something which inside, *without me knowing why*, <u>feels</u> right or good. And because that is true for me, it's true for others and that is why societies can agree on what is right and wrong.

What feels good to you is dependent on your chosen current experience. It is or can be different in each one.

But many other people I know feel the same as I do, right?

Because they have grown up with a similar life experience and agreed-upon series of historical events, laws, standards, traditions and/or beliefs.

But don't most societies have a common standard which would define good and bad deeds in a similar way?

Societies and civilizations have had and still have wildly different standards. For example, the Romans were entertained by slaughter and combat.

OK, but there are some core, common things that are agreed upon as "good"… Like helping someone in trouble, caring for children and the like. In fact, what I am getting at is that it FEELS good to do some things. So, isn't that an indication of what is right? If it feels good, it's right?

Some people do <u>not</u> feel good helping others and many don't want to be around children: The "goodness" of helping people and caring for children is defined by your prevailing social etiquettes. As we just said, what you feel as good varies on your chosen life experience. It's essential to note that even in your current life, some people like (feel good) hurting others.

Yes, but those people are unusual, aren't they?

Unusual? Is your measurement by your current moral and legal codes and the numbers of perpetrators who are caught and punished based on their breaking of those codes?

Yes, of course. But I guess there are those who are simply not caught… oh, and those who do not act on their evil preference or urges, I guess. But even then, these people are inherently evil, right?

They just are what they are.

What are you saying? That these people are OK?

Everyone is OK. They are doing what they are being.

Are your advocating evil and anarchy?

I am advocating nothing. I am stating what is.

Let me reference a story to try to explain what I mean: Charles Dickens' *A Christmas Carol.* **When I see Ebenezer Scrooge turn from a mean old curmudgeon to happy, generous man it feels good to me. It's the right ending - and I am left with a smile. So that's "good", right?**

It depends. Take other tales – from war to action to revenge stories - You also feel 'good' when the hero punishes or kills the opponent.

Yes but they <u>deserve</u> it ...because they *were* **bad.**

Ah - it feels good to you. Justice is done by the killing or brutalizing of another being. What feels good is usually whatever your mind believes is the achievement of the right end as you perceive it, <u>which is highly variable, based on your perspective:</u> The end justifies the means.

I see your point - but then sometimes guilt comes into play after the revenge is complete. Indeed, why would I feel guilty about taking revenge on the bad guy (even if it felt good at the time) if somewhere in the back of my mind I didn't know that what I did in the name of revenge is basically 'bad'?

You feel bad (or good) in hindsight of your actions only because of your social programming - your upbringing, religion, laws and societal norms. But those are only your own human mind truths – they are not of your larger Soul or beyond.

Let me come at this yet another way... Look at the people impacted by acts of others – many suffer <u>mental</u> as well as physical damage. If the result of an act is *psychological* **damage, then what was done must have been VERY bad because the individual is damaged at a subconscious level... Surely that's a fair definition of a truly bad act.**

Psychological harm and physical harm created by an action cannot be separated. They are a combined impact of that action. And both are as natural as the felling of a tree, the killing of an animal for meat, or the drowning of an ant in a rain barrel.

You are saying it's all OK then?

We are saying it just is.

But earlier you advocated peace and non-violence. So <u>those</u> things are good right?

Ultimately, we advocated *beyond* non-violence or 'peace' – we stated you need to know or do "no-thing". Such teachings are studied in *A Course in Miracles* and are core to the *Tao Te Ching*.

Wait a moment… so even <u>your</u> advice to me is not "good" or "right"?

It just is and from it you can do and create yourself as you wish.

Mmmm. I guess that's what you said all along: There is no wrong answer and no right answer – they are all, well, just *there*.

Everything just is.

So God is not good. Is God as evil as He is good?

Do you still imagine that God is anything like a man (or woman) to whom good and evil are such important polarities? God is the entirety of <u>everything</u> - of which your world and all its human history are one tiny, momentary possibility. And if God is everything, that means he is all things that you might label good, evil or anything else in your world. So, the conclusion that God is both good and evil is not a judgment or insult to God – it's an obvious fact if you believe God is (or even made) everything. But more importantly, we will repeat here that <u>you cannot explain God in human terms.</u>

Alright, so if we stay in human terms (which are my reality) is it not up to society to decide if an act is wrong and should be stopped or prevented?

First you need to remember that the practical world is not the truth – it is a place for your Soul to experience physical life and as such, cannot be used to explain greater truths - although they can be glimpsed like a ship through drifting fog. That said then, in the world as you perceive it, people on their own, and collectively as societies, do decide what acts are wrong and should be stopped or prevented based on what kind of society they desire. But those decisions are acts of human free will, not of God.

OK.

Now, you believe that society creates laws to keep you safe. But you can choose to live beyond those laws - it's up to you to decide if you want to judge anything or anyone. Remember we are not talking about changing this world in these dialogues: Try not to combine your world with the greater truth. As we have told you, you cannot understand the greater truth by trying to model it on your world, which, as you see it, needs laws to retain order. But the greater truth does not need rules and laws; only creativity. Since you want to think about this on a practical level, we have a question for you: You consider that laws protect good and the truth (i.e. that good and truth precede law). Is that true?

Yes. But are you about to suggest that things get swapped around - that law can (and therefore does) begin to define what is good and even the truth? And now I've said that I know it's true...

What is your experience with that?

I guess there's lots of evidence of it both in terms of legal outcomes as well as people who follow the law (or at least rules) *beyond* what might be regarded as the right thing to do or even the truth. Indeed, the very laws and rules designed to protect truths have

often been used to change the truths (and faiths) they were designed to protect.

So here is our message: The human conditions of good or bad are highly variable and even interchangeable. And if that is true, then good and bad do not exist as true constants, only temporary judgments. As the saying goes, the only constant is change – or more accurately, the only constant is creation. And as we told you earlier, God is all about <u>Creation</u> and here in your human world that means cycles of life and death, building and decay, growth and decline. What you define as good and bad are simply opposites - like up and down, left and right. They depend on perspective and one is no better than the other. *They are temporary, variable and totally subjective judgments of the essential polarities of Creation.*

OK, I get that in theory, but this is very difficult to *believe*. Why do so many teachings define an ultimate goal, then – either in this life or in the next: Such as 'peace on earth' and a loving heaven?

First we repeat that peace and love are worthy goals to you because that's what you consider good personally, at this moment, as do many others in your current social environment. Second we will say that attributes and behaviors such as peace and love help those in positions of power and responsibility to retain control and resources, and are therefore promoted (even if not displayed personally) by them.

Are you saying that the predominance of the goal of peace and love is not of God but simply one of societal leaders who see they have more stability and control under those conditions? But that can be said of terror and violence.

Behaviors attributed to "good" as you see it are typically more stable than those attributed to "bad". Terror and violence are less stable, and tend to be shorter lived.

So good and evil are merely intangible elements of this world

- to be used and manipulated like all its other el ments as part of creation... They are not core truths to which w should work towards or away from?

You can do with them whatever you wish.

Let me ask a related question then – should we not seek to destroy or end evil?

Can you destroy 'up' and keep only 'down'?

What do you mean?

Even if you could destroy 'up' and keep only 'down', there are two problems: First, 'down' would immediately cease to exist because it needs 'up' in order to be down. Second, by subsequently going 'down' in any way, you would immediately re-create 'up'.

Hold on. Good and evil are different to up and down aren't they? If I destroyed evil and left only good, that could be a maintainable state, right?

How would you know when you were done?

I'd have only good things left.

You would have only 'things' left. And in all things, there are some that are better (or more good) than others. You may have removed the extremes but you will be left with things – some of which will be more good (or less evil) than others. *You cannot eradicate the polarities.*

But if I kept whittling it down – wouldn't I ultimately find pure good?

You would find pure nothingness - for until you have nothing, you will always find polarities.

Mmmm... I think that last statement is a lot deeper than it first appears...

Let us conclude then. In your dimension, where there is down, there is up. Where there is good, there is evil. As we said earlier, this world is for God to experience everything that he is and is not. Now, perhaps we should clarify here that does not mean that your world is to provide an evil place so that a 'good' God can see what he is not. The whole world, good and evil is what He is not – simply He is not of this world in <u>any</u> way. Yet He is everything. He is beyond your understanding.

So God is not "good" then?

God is God. He enables us all to be. What we become in our worlds is up to us. Your world is a place of experiment and experience. It is one tiny piece of something beyond your comprehension in size and complexity. Work within this world, and your life, knowing this.

So is God about *peace* then?

Peace is a weighted word – it tends to be considered as an opposite to war, or a desired end state after conflict or chaos, noise or disturbance. <u>Consider "peace" as nothingness.</u>

Then there is no need to concern ourselves with pleasing God, of working hard and raising kids, of being good and defeating evil.

Only if that's what you want to experience.

Why not just be an evil and cruel person, or a lazy slob?

Because you choose not to be... most of the time.

Ouch. But where's the *reward*?

Ah – there's your need: To be told you are a good boy and will be rewarded. That need is the foundation of well behaved kids and of religions and most other organizations.

So, we are back to this all being about control by societal leaders. It just seems, well, like you're a conspiracy theorist!

What has been your experience in the underlying ambitions of leadership?

I have seen them do things I would call bad so as to maintain order, control and secure the 'greater good'. I thought there was always an underlying right thing to do - and leaders strove to do it. But it seems they don't.

Are you sure?

As much as I can be... but the point is that I don't always do the right thing all the time, do I?

You are learning...

Perhaps this world is just a reflection of me... or more importantly, what I fear I am or will be.

Don't become self critical here. You are aware of a greater truth. You are aware of your greater self - what you call your Soul and your purpose and role within it. You choose what you want to be in response to what you observe and experience. This is about you, as we have told you many times. Define the next highest version of yourself and what you want to be. The world will go on and you will influence it not by judging it but by observing it and responding to it differently as you create that higher version.

Before, I thought "higher" version of me meant better, nicer. But that's not it, is it?

It is, if that's what you desire. But whatever you seek to become, be it for you, not others, or even God. Be whatever you desire in this knowledge and allow the world and all those within it the freedom to do the same thing.

Review

1. God is everything – including our world and all its history. That means He is all things that we label good, evil or anything else. That's not an insult to God – it's a simple conclusion if you believe God is (or made) everything.

2. In our world, people and societies decide what acts are right and wrong based on the kind of society they desire or consider the norm. But those values are out of human free will, not dictums from God.

3. What we define as good and evil are simply opposites - like up and down, left and right. They depend on personal perspective and societal norms. "They are temporary, variable and totally subjective judgments of the essential polarities of Creation." A cursory review of the history of human civilizations shows this.

4. The goal of 'world peace' is not of God but one of societal leaders who have understood peace provides more stability than war – at least on the home front. While terror and violence can also yield control, they are more volatile and shorter lived approaches.

5. God is "peace" meaning the absence not of war but of <u>anything</u> in human terms: Think of the eternity of deep space; the sky at night.

CHAPTER 36

▼

The previous chapter was about there being no right or wrong or good or bad, which are simply judgments people make about what they experience. The same experience can be judged as either right or wrong dependent on the perspective of the person, society, time period or many other factors. If that is the case, there's no point in any of this, really.

What is your question?

What's the point of the human life if it's not to be good, to love one another?

To experience what the Soul desired.

Yes, I understand that. But I am struggling again with the thought that this seems to make this life nothing but a story in which I am a character.

The only difference between you and the character in a story or movie is that you have the opportunity to be 'aware'. Characters in fiction don't question the reality of their experience – they just have it, as defined by the author.

But the author could write the search for or experience of

'awareness' into the plot. In fact, many do – many characters are asking such things and seeking such answers.

But then THAT is the story from which they cannot deviate or escape. They are trapped within the story laid out before them and will always do, say and think what the author wrote each time the story is read. Because of this, they are never really questioning their reality and purpose.

But if I am just following the desired experience of my Soul, I am just the same, right?

There are two differences if you are aware and no longer only a 'Player': First, you are aware that the world experience you are having is not all there is, and second you are aware that there is only now and that you are choosing your next move in this instant. You are the character, the reader and the author all at the same moment.

Sounds like another version of the player-spectator-observer continuum. So the fact that I am truly 'aware' is the difference. That seems obvious of course.

But after what you have learned in these dialogues you understand (to a small extent at least) what that means. We also explained about free will earlier so we will not go over that again here.

I understand that right now I am <u>trying</u> to be an Observer. But I guess I feel that in reality, I am stuck as a character in my story.

And that is preventing you from fully observing. And that will be true while you seek for purely logical and finite answers.

Let me come at this from another angle: You have described that my free will is how I respond to the events which have largely been determined by my Soul's desired experience. So:

1. *Fatalism* **states that everything is predetermined – both effect and actions (i.e. any result <u>and</u> any actions that lead up to it or result from it are all predetermined). So you're not talking about fatalism here because you are saying I have a level of free will to respond based on my level of awareness.**
2. *Determinism* **states that only the** *result* **is predetermined – that my actions (and reactions) are free-willed and variable, but don't actually affect the end result.**

So, you are saying that determinism is closer to the truth, right?

Earlier, we explained that if you step back from all this worldly activity, you see a steady state, just as you see a solid rock from a distance but very close up there is space and activity at the atomic level. And in Chapter 34 we told you *"If you look at a photograph taken from space of a city on Earth, millions of individual events were occurring at the street level when the picture was taken, but you cannot see them in the image – but more importantly, they are not relevant in what you observe because the image exists as a complete and valid entity."* This statement is important here, too.

Why?

Because as we have told you, your human experience is the one desired by your Soul - which participates at a much higher level and of which you are a temporary manifestation with a particular experiential purpose. But <u>your</u> awareness level, Simon, is about <u>you</u> at the micro level. And at that level you have a great deal of influence (potentially at least). And that influence (and action) is an essential output of the Souls' intent.

I'm lost.

Your Soul (of which you are one tiny part), and all the others, collaborate in many ways and in many "dimensions" as you called them in your Personal Myth. All potentialities play out therein. Your reaction to your experiences, and your actions overall, can make a big difference to you and those immediately around you - or those in other countries if you are a Politician or a General, for example. You can influence things at any level of your world. However:

- If you stand back far enough, for example far enough to view the earth as a planet, your actions are not visible unless they are huge (such as creating a nuclear holocaust).
- If you stand further back, for example viewing your galaxy, even actions that do impact your world on a global level would be invisible and/or of little consequence.

I still don't understand how this answers if the truth is determinism, i.e. that my actions (and reactions) are free-willed and variable but don't really effect the end result.

Answer this question - What is the 'end result' to which you refer?

Why do you ask that?

We want you to understand that the "end result" depends on at what distance you are viewing things (or put another way, your perspective). If you are saying that your actions don't impact the "big picture" (e.g. things at, say, the galaxy level) then you are right. Nothing you can do can make an impact at that level given the huge scale. Indeed, can you imagine how insignificant you are if you move from galaxy level to other dimensions as you called them.

Yes.

Now, realize that you have free will to respond and act in any way and to have great influence in your human life. Here's the point: *The big picture is not irresistible or unchangeable by mankind in terms of a written pre-determined story by God, but rather in terms of the pure, incomprehensible, magnificent SCALE of God.*

So help me understand what that means to me.

It means that you can do as much or as little as you like. It means that there is no right and wrong, and that you can have no impact on the vastness of God. It means that you are <u>free</u> to play and discover what you are in the safety of knowing that.

...Because I am just a tiny feeble little thing!

In this life you can be a giant among men or a shrinking violet. The choice is yours. <u>And that is free will</u>.

But that's NOT free will!

What do you think "free will" is? Having great powers, and magical abilities to conjure health and wealth and to defy science and nature?

Well... good question. I guess free will means that you are not limited in any way.

Listen – free will is not about having power beyond yourself and your world. It's about not being afraid or limited by a fear of anything within or beyond your world and playing in it, with all its limitations, with the fearless, excited, awestruck joy of a child.

My head is spinning (as usual). So, assuming I understand all that (or will when I read it through ten more times) please talk to me about why this life is even *necessary*.

It's not. It just is.

That's not an answer.

What do you want to make of life?

Happiness I guess.

Go ahead then.

But to do that don't I need to believe that me, my life, is important, that my performance in it is how I am measured in some way, and that afterwards I will continue on in some form with another life which is better in some way as a result of my life here?

Sure - If you have traditional beliefs such as an overseeing God, heaven and hell, and Karma.

But I don't! We covered this in great depth already. In fact I don't know why I even asked that – it just came out.

It came out because it is there within you. And, at this moment you do believe it and it's a belief which has a deep root in you. It's an ingrained part of your perception of the world and your purpose based on your education, upbringing, generation and society.

Why is this so hard? I know (or try to remember) all you have told me and I agree with it... but I keep slipping backwards!

You agree with it *conceptually*, but you don't fully *believe* it. As Don Miguel Ruiz said, unless you truly believe then you remain only conceptually committed; you must dismantle your old beliefs before you can build anew.

What is holding me back?

Fear.

What am I afraid of... judgment, disapproval, damnation and hellfire I guess?

Yes – but that's not the root of it.

What is?

You are afraid of being wrong.

I can go with that. But is there really anything I can do about it? Is it hopeless?

There is no right or wrong. If there is no wrong then you have no need to be afraid of being wrong. If you can accept that, <u>even if only for brief periods</u>, then you can seek to build a new faith, one step at a time until those periods grow larger. Remember *A Course in Miracles* states "Make a place within you where the activity of the body ceases to demand attention. Into this place the Holy Spirit comes, and there abides..." Once you have done so, there is a place to which you can retreat to escape the noise and turmoil of the world.

How else can I help myself?

Don Miguel Ruiz gave sound advice when he suggested using "ritual". So, find ways to practice what you have learned here. Find ways and symbols to help you remember and most importantly replace your old programming.

That sounds like a religion to me!

Ritual is not religion, nor is religion a ritual. But ritual is used by religions for exactly the purpose we are suggesting – to help their followers *build their faith* in the religion.

That's a lot to take in. Summarize for me.

Understand your place in the oneness and vastness that is God. Use that knowledge to be free to be what you truly desire. Seek ways to break down the walls of fears and beliefs that limit you. You cannot go wrong; for whatever you do within YOUR FREE WILL (which is limited only by your imagination and bravery) is exactly what God intended.

I understand. Let me close this exchange referring to something my friend RC recently wrote to me in an email which loops back to our discussion earlier in this chapter about characters and authors. RC wrote:

> "*I think that we can find many truths in songs. Perhaps as they are being written the [songwriters] are accessing truth in their own way. But [according to what you have told me] there is no truth; there just is. I'm getting confused.*"

My response was this:

> "**It is said that** *beauty is in the eye of the beholder*. <u>**So is truth**</u>. **It exists only at the personal level. For example, I hear in songs (and observe) things which have meaning for <u>me</u> - or more precisely, <u>at this point</u> they are a truth for me. And my truths have changed and will probably change again.** "

Go on.

Perhaps there are 2 types of truth: Logical Truths and Inscrutable Truths:

- A Logical Truth is something that can be stated, written and explained - yet it's only a judgment in time, dependent on perspective and facts available, and therefore unstable. That is why, while it lasts, it requires constant justification and defending.
- An Inscrutable Truth is something that one simply feels is true... It is elusive; it cannot be described in words and needs no justification or defense. It is true "faith".

I think we get off track up when we try to make Inscrutable Truths into Logical Truths. Is that right?

You know better than to ask if it's the 'right' answer.

I guess so. But what do you think to what I wrote?

What you just created was an Inscrutable Truth... Until you wrote it down and made it Logical.

And that goes for this *whole book...*

Throughout these dialogues we have explained that logic was necessary for you to progress from the human you perceive yourself to be, to a new level of understanding. Indeed, this was essential as you developed this material, which, by its nature, needs to be logically organized and argued. But as we said earlier:

> *"You cannot know the truth, be given it, buy*
> *it, learn it or make it. You cannot describe*
> *it or write it. You can only experience and*
> *feel it. And only the truth is peace".*

Review

1. Free will is not about having power but about being unafraid of things within or beyond your world and living with the excitement and optimism you had as a child.

2. Find ways to practice what you learn so you can develop your emerging beliefs. For example use techniques and/or rituals to gradually replace your old programming.

3. Truth exists at the personal level and changes over time. God's truths cannot be explained using logic. They are inscrutable.

CHAPTER 37

▼

The hardest lesson in this work has been considering that God is neutral. Throughout history, people have believed that God is essentially good and benevolent, and that the human journey is to learn to be good and treat each other well, to love our brother, to live the Dharma and resolve the Karma. Such are the teachings of many masters.

We advise you to focus on what *you* desire to be in this life. It's what you truly believe and desire - even if you deny it - that manifests in your experience.

But what of all the teachings of goodness and love?

We have explained already about the true meaning of God's peace and the benefits to societies of using and promoting what you call good versus evil methods of power. But as we told you earlier, *"our guidance is about growth and change, not about perpetuation."* Expecting change while continuing to base your deepest beliefs on the religious traditions of history means you are continuing to do the same as before and expecting a different result.

But if the path to God is *not* goodness and love, why has God typically been assigned those attributes?

Gods have been assigned to specific things like skills, seasons or condition, including war and death. Your question comes from your Christian education and upbringing. And even then, the 'goodness' of the Christian God's desire to test, judge and sentence the majority of Souls to eternal hellfire for failing to meet His standards or exclusivity rules could be questioned.

But it would be argued that those old gods were false and that the one true God punishes only evildoers; as Christians and others such Ernest Holmes[14] put it "...we shall be obliged to suffer for the mistakes we have made. God does not bring this agony on us but we have imposed it on ourselves".

You could read that as saying that God punishes you (or at least lets you suffer) but it's your own fault for failing. But, if that's the case, consider this - The executioner is not guiltless in his duties; especially if he is also the rule maker, policeman and judge... which is hardly worthy of one all-loving, all-forgiving God. Therefore, we suggest that you interpret Holmes' statement as saying that God doesn't punish people and neither does he wish to – people suffer as a normal and expected part of their own actions/desires within the free will God provides. God has nothing to do with it directly.

Ok, but if we leave punishment out of it, there are many religions with their own God, and most of them seem to have basically the same expectations of their followers – show good behavior in life and earn a place in paradise. It's a great incentive. If God was to be declared neutral, wouldn't this world become a dreadful place?

Why?

Because people would behave badly (i.e. in ways most of us judge as bad and/or don't agree with) because there's no incentive to be good (or as you said above, there's no punishment for being bad).

14 Ernest Holmes (1887-1960) was the founder of Religious Science movement, also known as "Science of Mind", a part of the New Thought movement.

Many people already do behave what you call "badly".

I mean it would get even worse.

Would it? Would the world dissolve into chaos if someone said that God was neutral? Perhaps for those people who are confused at the lack of divine intervention to save lives and misery, it may explain why God does not step in.

But I think fear of God keeps a lot of people in line.

'Fear' of a good and kind God... an interesting paradox. But how do <u>you</u> feel about the possibility of a neutral God?

A little nervous...

Of what?

Of being wrong and facing damnation, I guess.

That's to be expected after living for over four decades with a fundamentally different perspective. Again, you said you think the world would get worse if God were to be neutral. But how do you feel about <u>yourself</u> and your life options with a neutral God?

Personally I still desire to be the things I wrote in Chapter 6: Healthy, positive, patient, open-minded, and guiding. And overall I still want to be considerate to others, and love my wife and children.

So why do you think other people would change for the worse?

I guess that's just my negative assumption about people. But surely there may be a few folks who would go off the deep end. For example, people who are on the edge of doing bad things, or people who live normal lives only because they believe they need to stay in God's favor.

People on the edge go over it for any number of reasons – they just need a reason or trigger to follow their true desire. And those who stay in line due to their fear of God would either not read this or just dismiss it as wrong and maybe get angry with you for suggesting it! Now, what else do you feel?

It's very *freeing* to think that God just intends me to experience what I came here to experience.

What's important is that your desires did not change for you with this new knowledge. And from now on, as you define higher versions of yourself they will be grander and freer as a result.

I see that now.

Review

1. A spiritual journey away from the traditional religion(s) on which most people grow up requires bravery. Base your bravery on the belief that God does not punish us for making wrong choices, and know that you can release any duty you feel to judge and punish others on His behalf.

2. We are here only to experience (and enjoy!) what we came to experience on behalf of God: It's not a pass/fail test.

3. Once you fully accept these simple truths, the higher versions you define of yourself (and seek to attain) will be grander and freer than you could ever have imagined before!

CHAPTER 38

▼

The next time I say (or hear) the term "God's creation" I will consider it means God IS creation - not that creation is something God owns or made.

As we have told you, God is everything, and as part of that, He is, as many believe, all love. Yet he is also all questions, doubts and fears, and even anger and hate. He is all that your mind judges on the continuums of right to wrong and good to evil.

Many will say that's blasphemy!

Those people will likely also say that God is the single and all powerful creator.

Yes.

If that is the case, then how can what we just said not be true? God really is <u>all</u> that is.

No, they would say that evil is from another entity – the Devil.

In that case, God would have made the Devil too. We discussed this earlier when we said:

> "And as part of creativity, there are not only new beginnings

and growth but also endings and destruction and change. *But there is no malevolence*, just constant creation and recreation... In nature there is life, and death, growth and decay all together, seamless, and it just is, peaceful and accepting amid even powerful natural upheavals and turmoil. This is God. He loves it all - not because it is "good" but because it is Him."

OK, but can you explain, perhaps in a way that helps me to understand what God is relative to me?

God is everything, including all questions, and that includes the question of 'what is HE?' And therefore, also the question 'what is He not?' You are a result of that and other questions. It is said that God created man in his own image. While that was a statement designed for human convenience, let's use it and consider now that instead of it meaning visual appearance or physical and personality attributes, it means like God in other ways – including your passion to create and develop and ask questions... including 'what am I?'

I know that's a big one for many people, but it's hardly a new concept!

OK. But now consider that you ask that question at every level of yourself - at your own human identity level (Simon), at your Soul level, and at every level of yourself inwards, from your body parts and organs to your cells, molecules and atoms.

What do you mean?

Do you remember the analogy we gave of you of putting your hand into fire to save your child and that your hand would do it even though it would be burned?

Yes. I said I expected, as part of me, my hand would do what was needed based on the overall decision that I was making with my

brain. And you explained the parallel between that and how I undertake my Soul's plan.

Indeed. You operate to the direction of a broader intent - your hand will do something that risks or actually hurts itself to do what your mind wants to do. Well, so will your mind do the same for your Soul.

Ok then. So, staying with your analogy, my hand cannot reach into the fire without the arm that moves it there.

Indeed - Your whole body collaborates in what needs to be done. And your whole body, as you perceive it at least, is made up of many different body parts and levels (skin, muscle, bones and below that, cells, molecules and atoms).

All the parts move to the orders without question?

That's a very important question... and our answer is No. They participate with questions just as your mind does... Including the one you ask about why "God" would want you to do certain things you don't like or make things happen around you (or to you) that you consider bad.

Wait - My *arm* questions things? My arm has no self awareness...

Not in the same way you think you do, but your understanding of your identity is wrapped up in your own belief in your independence and superiority of having a human brain. But it's all a matter of perspective and relativity; you're different, not superior.

I'm confused.

Sticking with the fire analogy, if you zoom-in on the arm during the fire, could you conceive that the *arm* at some level makes the decision to move the hand into danger?

Kind of – go on...

Now, zoom in again, and consider that the hand moves the finger into danger, and the finger the fingertip, and the fingertip the individual cell and so on? Unless compliance to the direction happens, the arm, finger or even skin would simply recoil away. Now, that can happen, but let's go with the general point here and consider this question: Who is really calling the shots?

I'm still confused.

Now zoom-out. Your body moves the arm, your brain moves the body, and your consciousness moves the brain.

But what moves my consciousness?

The next level...

My Soul! Then there is no independence... I am at the will (or mercy) of my Soul as much as my hand is at the mercy of my arm! I know we've been over this, but here you're explaining that ultimate direction always comes from the <u>next</u> level up – and after my Soul, well, ultimately it's GOD right?

There's more complexity to it and some of that we have already touched on, but that is a basic truth.

We truly are 'God's instruments' if you look at it like that. But tell me again where free will comes in...

Free will, in this analogy at least, comes at the <u>intersections</u> of each level (e.g. Soul to mind). At each intersection, there is the question of <u>how</u> the next level will respond to the direction it receives. At the intersection of the Soul to the mind, that is what you, Simon, typically refer to as "free will". It's what we have told you before.

OK.

What we will add now is that the level of flexibility (or awareness that an option is even present) depends on level of consciousness of the intersection; and your mind has a greater level of consciousness than, say your finger. We will also add that discomfort or illness in a specific body area is an indication that there is an intersection that is in conflict with the directions it has received. These conflicts can be below the mind level and are why illnesses do not usually seem to be something you, at the brain/ego consciousness level, would choose.

Boy, that's a bit hard to grasp. But if I understand you, it seems that ANY resistance to 'the plan' or divine direction is considered disobedience – and that sounds somewhat dictatorial to me.

Only if you consider discomfort or illness to be a bad thing, when it's actually only a helpful signal to which you can choose to respond.

I think I understand. One last question - which may sound a bit silly but is intriguing for me at least. Does each level see the one above it as its own "God"?

In a way - but not in the way that many people consider their God: As a controlling, overseeing, or parental character.

Again you remind me that I can't understand the bigger picture by defining it using the structures and limitations of the 'human condition' or experience. I get that, but the human condition is all I know – all I have been educated to believe and understand. So how can I truly understand what you are telling me?

Ah – there lies an important point. If you continue to try to understand using only the logic and models of your world, it's very hard to understand broader truths. You have to accept that you cannot fully understand it all. You must step from the edge of knowing into not knowing. That is the true leap of faith.

Religions often talk about the "leap of faith" needed to fully embrace them. Is that the same thing?

I am talking about a leap of faith not from one belief system to another, but from one belief system (i.e. your view of the world based on your belief system at that moment) to non-belief; To an open mind no longer building its interpretation and expectations of the world based on any one belief system, but a mind of acceptance and observation of what is. Accepting what one *feels* as much as understands.

Is that like being de-programmed or brain-washed then? Wiping all we have learned and been told to do (and not to do) from our childhood? In fact, is it like returning to our childhood state?

It is not that you should return to being a child (a relatively helpless state requiring learning of basic concepts to survive in your dimension) which would be impractical of course. But such a thought does recognize that a state of openness is possible because you had it earlier in your life. The task is to regain an openness of mind by dismantling old beliefs and reclaiming your faith.

Thank you. I will end this dialogue with a quote which provides what I think is an appropriate summary of your last point:

"In the beginner's mind[15] there are many possibilities, in the expert's mind there are few"

- Shunryu Suzuki, Zen
Master (1904-1971)

---

15 The "Beginner's Mind" is a term in Zen Buddhism and Japanese Martial Arts meaning to have the openness, eagerness, and lack of preconceptions of a beginner student, even when studying at an advanced level.

Review

1. There is consciousness at <u>every</u> level of our spiritual and physical selves - from our Soul level, to our human identity level (you, the reader), and at other levels inwards in your body... from your brain to your body parts and organs to your cells, molecules and atoms.

2. That consciousness has a degree of free will (just as you do from your Soul). The closer you remain to the direction and intent from "above", the more at ease you will be with your life, and the less 'dis-ease' you will experience. And that goes from aligning your consciousness with your Soul (spiritual fitness) to aligning your body with your brain (physical fitness).

3. A true leap of spiritual faith isn't stepping from one belief system to another, but shifting from a fixed belief system to an open mind or state of "non-belief". Claim your freedom of spirit - because "freedom comes <u>before</u> action".

CONCLUSION

▼

In Chapter 18, I developed a "Personal Myth" around which many concepts and spiritual ideas were explained and formed about what life and God may be all about; and that's what I set out to achieve. But here's the rub: The development of a personal myth or any other spiritual solution is not in and of itself our objective – and neither, so it turns out, is choosing a religion. The real objective is to achieve a state of being to which spiritual answers and religions are only stepping stones. Yet, every one of those stepping stones is valid and leads each of us, eventually, to the same place. But know this - that place is not a location, an ideal or an achievement. Instead, it's a still and watchful awareness that, all along, what you sought to find was there within you and needs no analysis, explanation, approval or justification. It just is, and awaits your remembrance of it. And once you accept that, you can truly "live the is that you have chosen".

Now, I am left with this conundrum: *Just how do I define a higher version of myself in the knowledge that I cannot do so using worldly artifacts?* My answer, at this moment at least, is this:

> In our role as the seeing eyes and the touching fingertips of God, it is through our *conscious* Observing that we can each discover our true purpose here, and thus define our higher selves.

I know Observing is hard to sustain - and for those who join me in whatever form their journey takes, I offer this advice: Temper your dignity in the heat of adversity you face on your journey: You serve God best by Observing the world, with complete presence, with forgiveness in each moment.

RECOMMENDED READING

▼

A Course in Miracles by Foundation for Inner Peace. Publisher: Viking Adult; 2nd edition (March 1, 1996) ISBN-10: 0670869759, ISBN-13: 978-0670869756

A New Earth by Eckhart Tolle. Publisher: Plume; Reprint edition (August 29, 2006), ISBN-10: 0452287588, ISBN-13: 978-0452287587

Awaken to Your Own Call by Jon Mundy: Publisher: Crossroad Classic (January 25, 1994) Language: ISBN-10: 0824513878 ISBN-13: 978-0824513870

Bringers of the Light by Neale Donald Walsch. Publisher: Hampton Roads Pub Co (June 1, 2000) ISBN-10: 0967875501, ISBN-13: 978-0967875507

Conversations with God Book 1 by Neale Donald Walsch. Publisher: Putnam Adult; 1st Hardcover Ed edition ISBN-10: 0399142789 ISBN-13: 978-0399142789

Creative Visualization by Shakti Gawain. Publisher: Full Circle Publishing Ltd (June 25, 2003) ISBN-10: 8176210625, ISBN-13: 978-8176210621

Do You Do It, or Does It Do You? by Alan Watts. Audio CD. Publisher: Sounds True; Unabridged edition (December 2005) Language: English ISBN-10: 1591793572, ISBN-13: 978-1591793571

Getting Unstuck by Pema Chodron. Audio Book. Publisher: Sounds True (November 30, 2004), ISBN-10: 159179238X, ISBN-13: 978-1591792383

Lazy Man's Guide to Enlightenment by Thaddeas Golas. Publisher: Devorss & Co ISBN-10: 0916108015 ISBN-13: 978-0916108014

Loving What Is by Byron Katie. Publisher: Three Rivers Press (December 23, 2003) ISBN-10: 1400045371, ISBN-13: 978-1400045372

Noble Heart by Pema Chodron. Audio CD Publisher: Sounds True; Package edition (October 30, 2004) ISBN-10: 1591792304, ISBN-13: 978-1591792307

Seth Speaks: The Eternal Validity of the Soul by Jane Roberts. Publisher: Amber-Allen, New World Library; Reprint edition (May 23, 1994) ISBN-10: 1878424076, ISBN-13: 978-1878424075

Recreating Yourself by Neale Donald Walsch. Publisher: Hampton Roads Pub Co (June 1, 2000) ISBN-10: 096787551X, ISBN-13: 978-0967875514

The Four Agreements by Don Miguel Ruiz. Publisher: Amber-Allen Publishing; Gift Ed edition (January 15, 2001) ISBN-10: 1878424505, ISBN-13: 978-1878424501

The Magical Approach by Jane Roberts. Publisher: Amber-Allen Publishing; New World Library (January 17, 1995) ISBN-10: 1878424092 ISBN-13: 978-1878424099

The Spontaneous Fulfillment of Desire by Deepak Chopra. Publisher: Three Rivers Press (August 12, 2004) ISBN-10: 1400054311 ISBN-13: 978-1400054312

The Voice of Knowledge by Don Miguel Ruiz. Publisher: Amber-Allen Publishing (April 2004) English ISBN-10: 1878424548, ISBN-13: 978-1878424549